STORIES OF THE PIONEERS

MEDIUMS, HEALERS & PSYCHICAL RESEARCHERS

THE GLASGOW ASSOCIATION OF SPIRITUALISTS

© 2024 by The Glasgow Association of Spiritualists

GAS PUBLISHING: ASSISTED BY SPOTLIGHT EDITORIAL

Copyright © 2024 by The Glasgow Association of Spiritualists

All rights reserved. No part of this publication may be reproduced, distributed or transmitted in any form or by any means, without prior written permission from the author organisation.

The Glasgow Association of Spiritualists/assisted by Spotlight Editorial
6/7 Somerset Place,
Glasgow, Scotland/UK G3 7JT
www.glasgowassociationofspiritualistssomersetplace.co.uk

Book Layout © 2016 BookDesignTemplates.com

© The Glasgow Association of Spiritualists 2024

Stories of the Pioneers: Mediums, Healers & Psychical Researchers
The Glasgow Association of Spiritualists (Charity No: SC005881) – 1st ed.
ISBN 9798332958410

Special thanks to

Dr Catherine McSporran and the Garnethill Writers' Group,
Carina Bryce of Spotlight Editorial, for donating the time and effort to typeset and guide the Church through the publishing process with Amazon,
&
All the pioneers of Spiritualism who worked so bravely to provide evidence to support the belief that consciousness survives physical death.

CONTENTS

Early History of Spiritual and Psychic Phenomena – The First Mediums _____10
Spiritual Connections _____12
Witchcraft versus Mediumship _____20
The Resurrection of Witchcraft: Helen Duncan _____24
Emanuel Swedenborg _____29
Andrew Jackson Davis _____33
The Fox Sisters _____36
Robert Owen _____44
Emma Hardinge Britten _____47
Davenport Brothers _____52
Eddy Brothers _____54
David Duguid _____57
Daniel Dunglas Home _____60
Reverend William Stainton Moses _____63
Madame d'Esperance: aka Elizabeth Hope _____67
Florence Cook _____69
Leonora Piper _____71
Reverend George Vale Owen _____74
John Campbell Sloan _____76
Edgar Cayce _____78
Gladys Osborne Leonard _____81
Rebecca Beard _____84
Frank Leah _____86
Estelle Roberts _____88
Eileen Jeanette Garrett _____93
Grace Cooke _____96
Harry James Edwards _____97
Anthony Borgia _____100
Maurice Barbanell _____102
Leslie Flint _____105
Albert Best _____111
Gordon Higginson _____115
Alfred Russel Wallace _____119
Sir William Crookes _____121

Henry Sidgwick	123
Frederic William Henry Myers	125
Sir William Fletcher Barrett	127
Edmund Gurney	130
Charles Richet	131
Sir Oliver Lodge	133
James H Hyslop	135
Sir Arthur Conan Doyle	137
Gustav Geley	141
Reverend Charles Drayton Thomas	142
James Hewat McKenzie	145
Hereward Carrington	147
Air Chief Marshall, Lord Hugh Dowding	149
Arthur Findlay	152
Professor Archie Edmiston Roy	154
The Glasgow Association of Spiritualists	156
Bibliography	166

Mediums and Healers

CHAPTER ONE

Early History of Spiritual and Psychic Phenomena – The First Mediums

Spiritual and psychic phenomena have occurred throughout the world since time immemorial. Ancient cultures often interacted with these energies, creating rituals and ancestral rites. Some viewed the phenomena with a mixture of terror and confusion, whilst others sought out and worshipped individuals for their powers of divination. These individuals have now been identified as history's first-ever mediums.

Far North and Arctic Native American Tribes: The Shamans

The Shaman was the most important person in each tribe or group. Shamans were paid for their work in food, hides and other items of value. The Shaman was not a medicine man. He was a mystical man. A Shaman was credited with many 'magical' powers. Through the power of chant and dance and magical signs and behaviour the people believed he could call up winds, interpret dreams, break up marriages and foretell the weather.

The early people of the far north believed in many magical beings. Some were good and some were evil. The Shaman had the power to talk to these magical beings and to direct their behaviour. Before hunters left to follow the herds, they consulted their Shaman, who used 'magical' aids to find the best path. First, a Shaman carved animal images on a piece of caribou bone. He heated the bone over a fire.

When it cracked, hunters were told to follow the lines to find the animals. Since animals were plentiful in ancient times, this method almost always worked. As in all far north tribes, the Shaman was the most powerful person. Interestingly, although we associate Shamanism with the North American Indians, experts have found evidence of Shaman practices in all six habitable continents of the world, dating back to the Paleolithic era (the early phase of the Stone Age).

CHAPTER TWO

Spiritual Connections

Guides and the North American Indians

Communications from the Spirit World have indicated that guides (helpers) may assist us in our day-to-day lives, and that they can appear in the form of North American Native Indians. If we take a look at the ancient North American tribes, we can see that their Ten Indian Commandments resemble our seven SNU (Spiritualists' National Union) Principles.

Ten Indian Commandments

1. Remain close to the Great Spirit.
2. Show great respect for your fellow beings.
3. Give assistance and kindness wherever needed.
4. Be truthful and honest at all times.
5. Do what you know to be right.
6. Look after the wellbeing of mind and body.
7. Treat the Earth and all that dwell thereon with respect.
8. Take full responsibility for your actions.
9. Dedicate a share of your efforts to the greater good.
10. Work together for the benefit of all Mankind.

Seven Principles of Spiritualism

1. The Fatherhood of God.
2. The Brotherhood of Man.
3. The Communion of Spirits and the Ministry of Angels.
4. The Continuous Existence of the Human Soul.
5. Personal Responsibility.
6. Compensation and Retribution Hereafter for all the Good and Evil Deeds done on Earth.
7. Eternal Progress Open to Every Human Soul.

Guides and the Ancient Egyptians (dating back to 3150 BCE)

As with the North American Indians, the Ancient Egyptians interacted with energies – and many appear as modern-day guides. In ancient times, the Egyptians called upon priests of the highest order to determine matters ranging from war and harvest to life after death. The priests would oversee the mummification and burial rites, even placing special 'spells' and 'curses' within tombs to protect the inhabitant.

The Ancient Chinese

The ancient Chinese also interacted with energies. They believed that after someone died, their spirit lived on in the 'After-World'. From there, the spirits of family members were able to watch over you. Family spirits included all of your ancestors, going back generations, who were believed to be able to help you, or hurt you, making ancestor veneration a common practice.

Oracle Bones (or, Dragon's Bones) were used in the Shang Dynasty of China (c. 1600-1046 BCE) for divination. These bones were the shoulder blades of oxen, or plastrons of turtles (the flat underside of the turtle's shell). A fortune-teller would carve (later, paint) symbols on the bones of the ox, or the turtle shell, apply a hot poker, or fire, until the bone or shell cracked, and then interpret the direction of the crack through their drawing to predict the future.

Taoism of Ancient China: how it compares to Spiritualism

Just as our guides and helpers might manifest as North American Indians and Ancient Egyptians, they can also appear as the ancient wise men from China. If we take a look at Taoism of Ancient China, we can see why. The word Tao means path or way. Tao is the absolute principle underlying the Universe, combining within itself the principles of yin and yang, and signifying the way, or code of behaviour, that is in harmony with the natural order.

Within Taoism is a path, so nothing we are learning today is new to anybody in the Spirit World. Everything has been done and tried over many generations; and the many generations within the Spirit World are able to come back and help us to understand the path that we have all taken through our life – not just our physical lives but also through our eternal lives.

The Oracles (fortune-tellers) of Greece and Rome: The Sibyls

Sibyls (female prophetesses) were first mentioned by the ancient Greek writer Heraclitus in 500 BCE. They were a class of women who gave prophecies whilst in a state described as 'frenzied' or 'ecstatic'. Psychical researchers say that this state is similar to what some mediums pass through prior to making contact with their spirit guide. Evidence shows that the practice of being a Sibyl may well date back to 2,000 BCE. The last prophecy of the Oracle of Apollo (at Delphi), took place in 392 CE after the Roman Emperor Theodosius ordered the closure of all 'pagan' sanctuaries.

Tibet

Mahasiddha Virupa is one of the famous eighty-four great Indian Masters. He is believed to have practiced a form of mystical divination through disciplined meditative study and attained great realisations in one lifetime. His reported 'wisdom' continues to influence those seeking spiritual attainment – particularly followers of the Sakya School, which is one of four major schools of Tibetan Buddhism.

Evidence of Psychic Phenomena in the Bible

Examples of supernatural powers can be seen frequently in the Bible. It is very discerning, however, as to who can manifest such powers. The Hebrew people were told to avoid false prophets and consult the good ones. Indeed, some psychic abilities were classified as gifts of the Holy Spirit. If we look further at the Bible, and indeed, other religious books, we will see that there have been many teachers. But these teachers who have come and departed from the physical world, have been given many labels by humankind. Jesus came to spread the word of love as *a* child of God: not *the* son of God. Jesus was *not* a Christian, and similarly, Buddha was *not* a Buddhist. They were teachers and healers and came to the physical world to spread words of wisdom, love and light.

Scotland

Finally, let us not forget the Scottish homeland: the land of seers, second sight and divination. First, let's take a look at the Brahan Seer. According to legend, he was a seventeenth-century predictor of the future. He is thought to have used an adder stone, that is, a stone with a hole in the middle, to see into the future. He predicted many things.

1. The time would come when Culloden would become a battlefield, where many would suffer violent death. The Battle of Culloden took place in 1745.
2. Scottish lochs would join together. This was accomplished by the construction of the Caledonian Canal in the nineteenth century.
3. There would be horses spitting out fire. More than two hundred years later, railways were built through the Highlands.

4. The discovery of North Sea oil in Aberdeen. He called the oil 'black rain'.

The Brahan Seer also spoke of the day when Scotland would once again have its own parliament. This would only come at a time when the English and French could cross into each other's borders by land. The opening of the Channel Tunnel in 1994 was followed a few years later by the opening of the first Scottish Parliament since 1707.

Many debates have resulted regarding the accuracy of the predictions. Where SNU Spiritualism is concerned, communications are usually made with the Spirit World to provide evidence of past and current events – and to prove to the sitters that the communicators from the Spirit World are who they say they are. Although mediums are not encouraged to predict the future, events have been known to be predicted. This is well illustrated in the case of the medium WT Stead, who was warned on several occasions not to cross on the Titanic. He ignored these warnings to his cost.

Folklore

The Scots have always been well known for being part of a culture enmeshed in folklore, which should not be confused with Spiritualism.

Bean-Nighe: A mythical 'washer woman'. Legend has it she can be found by streams and pools, washing the clothes of those who are about to die.

Selkie: Mythical shape-shifting creatures that can turn into seals and beautiful people.

Kelpies: Fanciful creatures that can take the shape of beautiful horses that appear near rivers and lakes. They entice people to ride them and take their riders down to a watery grave.

Storm Kelpies or the Blue Men of the Minch: Blue skinned creatures that are said to swim right below the surface of the water between

Lewis and the Scottish mainland looking for boats to sink and sailors to drown.

Loch Ness Monster: And of course, we have the Loch Ness Monster. The first sighting was in 565 CE by St. Columba when he saw a huge monster swimming towards one of his servants. There have been many more sightings; unfortunately, at least three photographs have been proven to be fake. But the truth of the matter remains a moot point. In 1991 Dr David Bellamy (naturalist) commented that although it would be nice if it was real, no one should be allowed to know its whereabouts because they would probably harm it.

Ghosts and Legends

Scotland abounds with stories and legends, begging the question: what is fact and what is fiction? So, let's do a bit of research by taking a look at some of the better-known examples of 'ghosts' and 'spectres' in the houses, castles and ruins of haunted Scotland. Hopefully then, we will start to dispel some of the more obvious myths and legends and learn a bit more about the facts.

Blackness Castle, Falkirk

The castle was built in the fourteenth century, and massively strengthened in the sixteenth century. It became an artillery fortress, a royal castle, an armaments depot and a state prison. The central tower is known as the 'Prison Tower'. To get to the top, you climb a winding stone staircase, and it is here that a knight in armour has been seen. Noises have also been heard: usually furniture being scraped and banged across a stone floor.

Mary King's Close, Edinburgh

Mary King's Close is buried beneath the eighteenth-century buildings of the City Chambers. Those who once lived in its squalid and rat-infested tenements often became victims of the Plague.

In 1645, the Plague returned with a vengeance and the close was walled off, confining its residents to a horrible death. Once the pestilence had abated, the stench from the corpses became unbearable. Two butchers were sent in, and they hacked the rotting bodies and wheeled away the parts. Unsurprising then that sightings have been made of earth-bound spirits of the deceased.

More recently, a Japanese medium was brought over by a television company. She knew nothing of the history of the Close, but when she stepped into one of the rooms, she was struck by a disturbingly depressive ambience. As she turned to leave, someone tugged at her trouser leg. She went back into the room and found the spirit of a young girl in the corner. The girl identified herself as one of the victims of the Plague in 1645.

Balgonie Castle, Fife

This is the residence of the Laird of Balgonie. It is a fourteenth-century tower, and was probably built by Sir Thomas Sibbald, Lord High Treasurer of Scotland, but was added to and expanded over the centuries. The spirits of humans and animals have been seen walking around the castle – and mediums have detected cold spots. Probably the most famous spirit is 'Green Jeanie', who, since the nineteenth century, has been seen in her green attire, her face concealed by a hood, walking behind the iron bars of the ground floor windows.

Dalzell House, Lanarkshire

This is one of the finest mansions of the Scottish Lowlands. It consists of a mix of buildings clustered around a fifteenth-century tower house, which has a history of bloodshed and war. The house is also said to be haunted. The 'green lady' is a spirit that wanders the south wing of the building. The 'grey lady' prefers the north wing, and the 'white lady' appears from time to time in different parts of the property. All are believed to have history with the house.

Traquair House, Scottish Borders

Traquair House has played host to twenty-seven Scottish monarchs, including Mary Queen of Scots and Bonnie Prince Charlie. The House has survived a tumultuous and emotional past, and there have been sightings of ghosts in its grounds: including the spirit of Lady Louisa Stewart, sister of the ninth Earl of Traquair, and the last Stewart lady to live there.

Ravenswood House, Aberdeenshire

This is the home of two resident ghosts, who wander the interior of the property, now a hotel. The first ghost is believed to be the spirit of the original owner, who erected the property in 1820. The second ghost is the spirit of a nanny, who appears when young children come to stay.

The Prince's House Hotel, Glenfinnan

The Prince's House Hotel dates back to 1658 when it started life as a change house, providing shelter and fresh horses for travellers – and at least two ghosts are known to haunt it. One is the spirit of a grey lady who has been sighted on the stairs. The other is the spirit of a bearded highlander, who occasionally wanders the building.

Seers, Witches, Sensitives and Mediums

So, seers, witches, sensitives and mediums: what is the difference? These are names attached to men and women (even children) with the ability to connect with the Spirit World. As for the ghosts, spirits, phantoms, apparitions and spectres: these are, fundamentally (although not necessarily always), representations of what is left of once 'living' people, who can connect with us (or, appear unknowingly to us) in the physical world, mostly through love, but sometimes through fear, sadness and any other kind of deep emotion.

CHAPTER THREE

Witchcraft versus Mediumship

Witchcraft

The Cambridge Advanced Learner's Dictionary states that Witchcraft is *'the activity of performing magic to help or harm other people'*. This encompasses the idea of a witch on a broomstick communicating with the Devil, and totally discounts the practices of today's white witches, who claim to only use magic to do good things.

Witchcraft in Western Europe and America

In the Middle Ages, Witchcraft was deemed to be heresy throughout Western Europe. In 1484 it was denounced as such by Pope Innocent VIII. It became a capital offence in Britain in 1563. Between 1484 until around 1750 some two hundred thousand 'witches' were burned or hanged after undergoing appalling torture. During the late seventeenth century, the Puritans of New England in America, began a series of prosecutions (most notably in Salem), during the course of which, many people were accused of practising Witchcraft. Eventually the public began to realise that innocent people were being condemned to death, and the process was forced to cease.

Joan of Arc: clairaudience and clairvoyance

One of the most famous examples of clairaudience and clairvoyance can be found in the case of Joan of Arc. Joan was born to a peasant family at Domrémy, northeast France, around the year 1412. From the age of thirteen years, she received 'divine guidance' through clairaudience, and 'visions' through clairvoyance, which led her to believe that the voices belonged to the Catholic saints: Michael, Margaret and Catherine. Joan believed that the voices carried messages from God, directing her destiny and foretelling her future. They told her that in 1429 she would lead an army to fight the English in the besieged city of Orleans, and that she would be wounded in battle. Both these predictions came true.

The voices went on to tell Joan that she would find a sword buried near the altar of the Church of Saint Catherine at Fierbois. It would be covered in rust, but once cleaned, would have five crosses inscribed on its blade. Joan asked the priests of the village church to unearth the sword – which they did. When they cleaned the rust off the blade, they found it was inscribed with five crosses, as Joan had predicted. Unfortunately, French rebels handed Joan over to the English. In 1431, she was tried by an ecclesiastical church, which convicted her of Witchcraft and heresy, whereupon, she was burned at the stake.

Nostradamus

Nostradamus was the famous French Seer of the 1530s. He was able to make predictions by looking into a bowl of water. But Nostradamus had to be careful. He lived at a dangerous time. The Church had an incredible hold over the minds of the people, and mediums and sensitives were always in fear of being branded as sorcerers. Most lived in fear.

At the age of fifteen, the young Nostradamus entered the University of Avignon, but was forced to leave when the University closed its doors because of plague. From 1521, he travelled the countryside, researching herbal remedies. In 1545 he assisted the prominent physician, Louis Serre, in his fight against a major plague outbreak in Marseilles. He then tackled further outbreaks in Salon-de-Provence and Aix-en-Provence.

In 1550 Nostradamus moved away from medicine and began to write his almanacs. Combined, they contain over six thousand prophecies. He then embarked on a book of one thousand quatrains, foretelling the future. These were four-lined rhymes designed to try and fool the religiously fervent authorities of the time. They were published in a book entitled: *Les Propheties* (The Prophecies).

Some individuals thought Nostradamus was a servant of evil, a fake, or insane, whilst many of the elite thought his quatrains were spiritually-inspired prophecies. Most of the quatrains deal with disasters such as plague, earthquakes, wars, floods, invasions, murders, droughts and battles. But some of his prophecies have proved significant.

1. He is believed to have predicted the rise of Hitler in 1933.
2. Also, the assassination of President John F Kennedy in 1963.
3. More recently, many believe he predicted the outbreak of the coronavirus pandemic (Covid-19).

It is thought that Nostradamus was afraid of being persecuted for heresy by the Inquisition. Fortunately, prophecy and astrology did not fall into this bracket. He would only have been in danger had he practised magic to support them. In fact, it turned out that his relationship with the Church as a prophet and healer was excellent.

The last 'witch' to be executed in the British Isles

The last 'witch' to be executed in the British Isles was Janet Horne. There is dubiety as to whether this was in 1722, or 1727. Janet was from Scotland. She and her daughter were arrested in Dornoch (Sutherland) following claims of Witchcraft by their neighbours.

Horne was showing signs of senility, and to make things worse, her daughter had deformed hands and feet. The neighbours accused Horne of using her daughter as a pony, and riding her to visit the devil. The trial was quick, and both women were found guilty and sentenced to be burned at the stake. The daughter managed to escape, but Janet was stripped and smeared with tar, then paraded through the town on a barrel and burned alive.

There is further dubiety as to whether Janet was Horne's real name. Janet (or Jenny) was a generic name used for witches in the north of Scotland at the time. It is quite possible that contemporary writers did not know her real name, and decided to use the next best thing.

The Witchcraft Act 1735

Although severe, the Witchcraft Act did, in fact, abolish the hunting and execution of 'witches' in Great Britain. The maximum penalty set out by the Act was a year's imprisonment. Nonetheless, it was frequently invoked in the early years of the nineteenth century in an attempt by the political elite to root out 'ignorance, superstition, criminality and insurrection' among the general populace.

CHAPTER FOUR

The Resurrection of Witchcraft: Helen Duncan

(1897–1956)

By the twentieth century, one would have thought that public interest in 'Witchcraft' was well off the radar. The case of Helen Duncan proves that this was not the case.

Background

Helen was born on 25 November 1897 in the small Scottish town of Callender. She married Henry Duncan, who had been injured during the First World War, and was unable to work. With six children to support, Helen became the family bread winner. By day she worked in a local bleach factory, and conducted her spiritual and domestic duties at night.

Helen was a physical medium who could produce ectoplasm, whilst in trance. Harry Price, a well-known psychical researcher of the time, accused her of fraud, claiming the ectoplasm was, in fact, cheesecloth that had been hidden in her body orifices. In the early 1930s she was put on trial in Scotland and fined for falsely claiming to communicate with the dead.

During the Second World War, Helen and her family were living in the Naval City of Portsmouth, where her services as a medium were in great demand. Families were losing loved ones, and were desperate to make contact with them.

In November 1941, during a séance, Helen brought forward the spirit of a sailor, wearing a Royal Navy hatband with the name *HMS Barham*. The sailor announced: *'My ship is sunk.'* Unbeknown to the British public, a few days before the séance, *HMS Barham* had been torpedoed by a German U-boat and sunk off the coast of Egypt.

Interestingly, at the time of the incident, the commander of the U-boat (Hans-Diedrich von Tiesenhausen) remained unaware of *HMS Barham's* identity. He radioed his superiors stating he had torpedoed a battleship with unknown results. When British code-breakers intercepted this message, the British authorities decided to hold back on announcing the disaster for fear of demoralising the British people. It was also another way to keep the enemy in the dark. Unfortunately, there remained a problem.

Helen's unwitting intervention had spoiled the plans of the British Admiralty. They feared her séances would unravel their extensive measures of concealment. They decided not to arrest her at that time, but kept a very close watch on her spiritual activities. One evening in January 1944, when Helen was conducting a séance in a private home in Portsmouth, matters took a turn for the worse. Undercover naval officers and police officers had infiltrated the meeting. When Helen produced ectoplasm, the infiltrators blew a whistle, and assuming this to be cheesecloth, tried to grab it; but it disappeared when someone switched on the lights.

When the 'cheesecloth' could not be found, the infiltrators agreed that someone must have hidden it about their person. Helen and three others were thereupon arrested and charged with vagrancy before the Portsmouth magistrates.

Then things got worse.

Higher authorities intervened, and Helen was taken to London to face charges from the Director of Public Prosecutions. The more serious accusation of conspiracy, punishable by death in wartime, replaced the original infraction. Finally, the prosecutors decided to charge her with violating the 1735 Witchcraft Act. Helen was indicted on seven punishable counts: two of conspiracy to contravene the Witchcraft Act; two of obtaining money by false pretences; and three of public mischief: a common law offence.

Helen's trial at the Old Bailey began on 23 March 1944. It lasted a week, during the course of which, the prosecutors introduced evidence relating to *HMS Barham*, highlighting that Helen had disclosed information that should have remained an Admiralty secret. In the end, the jury found her guilty of a conspiracy to violate the Witchcraft Act on the grounds that she had claimed to summon spirits. It is often contended that her imprisonment was, in fact, ordered at the behest of superstitious military intelligence officers, who feared that she would reveal the secret plans for D-Day. She was sentenced to nine months in London's Holloway Women's Prison. Unfortunately, Helen was plagued with a lifetime of ill-health, and her term in prison did not help. She died in 1956.

HMS Barham

In 1957 a group of *Barham* veterans founded the *HMS Barham Survivors Association*. At one of their reunion dinners held in Portsmouth, they had a surprising visitor: Commander Hans-Diedrich von Tiesenhausen, who had gone on to survive the war as a prisoner. In 1998 he was told the story of Helen Duncan. He reportedly replied: 'No government should be allowed to treat a poor woman so terribly.'

Such is the legacy of Helen Duncan.

Was Helen Duncan the last person to be indicted under the Witchcraft Act?

The answer is: *no*.

The last person convicted under the Act was Jane Rebecca Yorke of Forest Gate in East London. Yorke had worked as a medium for many years. She was prosecuted by police in 1944 because of claims she was defrauding the public by exploiting wartime fears. On 26 September 1944 at the Central Criminal Court, Yorke was convicted on seven counts of *'pretending to cause the spirits of deceased persons to be present'*. She was fined £5 and placed on good behaviour for three years, promising she would hold no more séances. The light sentence was due to her age of seventy-two.

Fraudulent Mediums Act 1951 and the Vagrancy Acts

Thomas Judson Brooks played an instrumental part in making the Government repeal the Witchcraft Act, and have it replaced with the Fraudulent Mediums Act 1951. Brooks was a British coal miner and politician, who became a Labour Party Member of Parliament – and also a Spiritualist. He was born on Eastfield Farm at Thurgoland near Barnsley, Yorkshire, however, instead of following his father into farming, he became a coal miner at Glass Houghton. Active in the Yorkshire Mine Workers' Association, he became Secretary of his branch of the Union in 1911. He then entered politics, rising up the ranks, until he was elected Labour Member of Parliament for Rothwell in 1942.

In 1943, Brooks conveyed a delegation of representatives of the Spiritualists' National Union (led by Air Chief Marshal, Lord Dowding, head of Fighter Command during the Battle of Britain in 1940) to the Home Office, where they presented a case for the removal of various provisions of the Vagrancy Act. The Act had first been put into place in 1824, to control the number of beggars and homeless, who were mainly casualties of earlier wars. It had been amended several times, most notably by the Vagrancy Act 1838, which introduced a number of new public order offences, covering acts that were deemed at the time to be likely to cause moral outrage. This was followed by the Vagrancy Act 1898, which although intended to deal with soliciting and importuning for immoral purposes, namely prostitution, was also being applied to cases of mediumship.

Brooks and his delegation were unsuccessful at this time. They were told by the Home Office that private members' bills had been suspended for the duration of the war, so any change was impossible.

By 1951, the decision was reversed. A bill was drawn up to repeal the Witchcraft Act 1735, and replace it with an act that would criminalise deliberate deception. With Brooks' guidance, the Fraudulent Mediums Act 1951 was passed unanimously. It prohibited a person from claiming to be a psychic, medium, or other spiritualist while attempting to deceive, and to make money from the deception.

Consumer Protection from Unfair Trading Regulations 2008

On 26 May 2008 the Fraudulent Mediums Act was repealed by Schedule 4 of the Consumer Protection from Unfair Trading Regulations 2008, which makes it an offence for a person to purport to act as a spiritualist medium with intent to deceive. The Regulations also provide a mechanism for a refund, if unsatisfied with services received.

CHAPTER FIVE

Emanuel Swedenborg

(1688–1772)

Emanuel Swedenborg was a Swedish scientist, philosopher, theologian – and medium.

Early Life and Works

The young Swedenborg graduated from the University of Uppsala in 1709. Fascinated by mathematics and the natural sciences, he spent the next few years travelling in England, Holland, France and Germany, where he was introduced to the new sciences, and learned practical mechanical skills. His inventiveness and mechanical genius developed at this time, and amongst his ideas were methods of constructing docks, and tentative suggestions for the submarine and aeroplane. Swedenborg returned to Sweden in 1715, and began to publish a scientific journal called *'Daedalus Hyperboreus'*. Here he described his projects and discoveries.

He was soon appointed to the position of assessor at the Royal Board of Mines, where he devoted himself to the development and improvement of Sweden's metal mining industries. Swedenborg went on to publish reports and treatises on various scientific and philosophical problems, which included cosmology. Always interested in mathematics, in 1718, he published the first work on algebra in the Swedish language. He also studied human sensory perception.

Swedenborg's philosophy of nature

In 1721 Swedenborg travelled abroad for the second time. He published two Latin volumes on natural philosophy (natural sciences) and chemistry. In 1722 he stopped writing, and for the next ten years worked quietly in his role as a civil servant. In 1733 he set out on a third European tour. When he was in Leipzig (Germany), he published *Opera Philosophica et Mineralia* (Philosophical and Logical Works). This comprises three volumes, and contains Swedenborg's philosophy of nature. It concludes that by using analytical reasoning, matter consists of particles, which are indefinitely divisible, and these particles whirl around in constant motion. Moreover, these particles are themselves composed of smaller particles, also in motion. Interestingly, this is not dissimilar to today's knowledge of particles, which make up atoms, in particular, the spinning motion of electrons.

Swedenborg becomes interested in the human soul

Swedenborg returned to Sweden, but when his father died in 1735, he decided to go back to Europe. In Amsterdam, he published a new work, in two volumes: *Oeconomia Regni Animalis* (the Economy of the Animal Kingdom), which examined the human body, but not as a single subject. He wanted to prove the immortality of the soul. His work made a thorough study of human anatomy and physiology, with special attention to the blood and brain. He collected his facts from experimentalists and microscopists, and from this information, drew up his own conclusions, which included the identification of areas of the brain impacting on mental health. Unfortunately, the scientists of the time showed no interest in his anatomical work. When finally, it was uncovered in the nineteenth century, science had advanced too far to make any use of it.

Swedenborg's religious crisis

In 1741, when he was fifty-three years of age, Swedenborg began to have strange dreams and visions. In 1745, whilst dining in a private room in a London tavern, his vision darkened, and he saw someone sitting in the corner. The person turned to him and warned him to be sparing with what he ate. Swedenborg became afraid, and hurried home. Later that night, the same man appeared in Swedenborg's dreams. He told him that he was the 'Lord', and that he had appointed Swedenborg to reveal the true spiritual meaning of the Bible. He would guide Swedenborg in what to write.

From that day, the Spirit World opened up to Swedenborg. He was able to visit 'Heaven' and 'Hell' where he conversed with the 'Angels' for twenty years. Between 1749 and 1771 he wrote thirty volumes, all of them in Latin, and mostly anonymously. These included: *Arcana Coelestia* (Heavenly Arcana), and *Apocalypsis Explicata* (Apocalypse Explained). The works gave accounts of his spiritual interpretation of Bible verses in Genesis, Exodus and the Book of Revelation. In 1758, he wrote: *De Coelo et ejus Mirabilibus et de Inferno* (On Heaven and Its Wonders and on Hell), and in 1771, *Vera Christiana Religio* (True Christian Religion).

It is believed that his spiritual senses were awakened so he could experience both the Spirit World and physical world, and allow God to tell him of a new age of truth and reason in religion. Although he was a medium, his dry matter-of-fact accounts of the Spirit World, and his logical reasoning, show that he retained the qualities of both a scientific and philosophical investigator. He consistently believed that the infinite power of life within Creation, is God. He further claimed that the true order of Creation was disturbed by man's misuse of his free will. Man had diverted his love from God to his own ego, so allowing evil to come into the world.

He believed that in order to redeem and save mankind, the divine being of God had to come into the world in the material, tangible form of a human being: Jesus Christ. This is still the Christian belief. However, a major difference between SNU Spiritualism and Orthodox Christianity is embodied in Spiritualism's fifth principle: Personal Responsibility. Jesus is *a* son of God, as we are all children of God, and Jesus was a great medium, a healer and a wonderful teacher. SNU Spiritualists cannot accept, however, that he died to save us from our sins. Personal responsibility means we are accountable for our own sins. We are given free will, and are responsible for all our thoughts and actions. We are our own judges here and now, and we shall receive compensation or retribution for whatever we have done, whether good or bad. Heaven and Hell are not places to which we are destined to go, but states of mind of our own creation.

Fire Anecdote

On Thursday, 19 July 1759, a great and well-documented fire broke out in Stockholm. The strong wind made it spread very fast, consuming about three hundred houses, and rendering two thousand people homeless. During the fire, Swedenborg was at a dinner with friends in Gothenburg, which is about four hundred kilometres from Stockholm. At 6pm, he became agitated, and told the party that there was a fire in Stockholm, and that it had consumed his neighbour's home, and was threatening his own. Two hours later he exclaimed with relief that the fire had stopped three doors from his house. At that time, it took two to three days for news to reach Gothenburg from Stockholm by courier. The first messenger from Stockholm with news of the fire was from the Board of Trade, who arrived on the Monday evening. A second courier (Tuesday) arrived with news. Both reports confirmed everything Swedenborg had said.

CHAPTER SIX

Andrew Jackson Davis

(1826–1910)

Andrew Jackson Davis was the founder of the Spiritualists' Lyceum Movement.

Background

Davis was born in Blooming Grove (Orange County), New York. His father was a cobbler and weaver. His mother, although illiterate, was very religious. The family frequently moved around, so Davis had very little schooling. His first job was as apprentice to a shoemaker, which lasted 2 years.

Mesmerism

In 1838, the Davis family moved to Poughkeepsie, New York. In 1843, Davis attended a lecture on Mesmerism. Mesmerism is a hypnotic state, induced by the imposition of the hypnotist's will on that of the patient. It is also known as Animal Magnetism and Magnetic Trance, and was given this name by the Austrian doctor, Franz Anton Mesmer, who was an eighteenth-century physician.

Mesmer said all living things, including humans, animals and vegetables, have an invisible natural force, which can have physical effects. He believed that the distortion of this force round the body was responsible for all suffering, and that this could be countered and cured by placing magnets on a patient's body, or using magnetised water. Practitioners of his methods were known as magnetisers. Hundreds of books were written on the subject between 1766 and

1925, and although almost entirely forgotten today, it is still practised as a form of alternative medicine in some countries.

Davis experiments with Mesmerism

Davis began to experiment with Mesmerism, but experienced little success, until William Livingston, a local tailor (also experimenting with Mesmerism), threw Davis into a trance – and matters developed from there. Livingston was able to use Davis's clairvoyant powers for the diagnosis of disease. As Davis's clairvoyance (seeing Spirit) and clairsentience (sensing Spirit) developed, his ability to go into trance intensified. He became known as the 'Poughkeepsie Seer', and he referred to his altered states of consciousness, as the 'superior condition'.

Trance Orations

In 1844, whilst in a state of semi-trance, Davis was inspired to go to the Catskill Mountains, where he had an in-depth discussion with two materialised spirits about medicine and morals. One spirit was later identified as Aelius Galenus (Galen), physician, surgeon and philosopher at the time of the Roman Empire. Arguably the most accomplished of all medical researchers of antiquity, Galen influenced the development of various scientific disciplines, including anatomy, physiology, pathology, pharmacology and neurology, as well as philosophy and logic. He was also the first scientist and philosopher to assign specific parts of the soul to locations in the body.

The other spirit was Emanuel Swedenborg (see previous chapter), the eighteenth century theologian, mystic, scientist and philosopher, who claimed to have conversed with the 'Angels' over a period of twenty years. On another occasion, Davis gave a trance oration in the presence of Dr George Bush, who was Professor of Hebrew. Bush confirmed that Davis's discussions about historical and biblical archaeology were of a high standard. Since Davis's own education was poor, it was determined that he was being used as a conduit by the Spirit World.

Lyceum

On 25 January 1863, Davis addressed a Spiritualist audience at Dodsworth Hall. He described a vision he had had during one of his altered states of consciousness: spirit children being taught and trained in the Spirit World. He suggested that a similar system of learning could be of great benefit to children on the earth. This inspired members of the audience to meet and establish the first Children's Progressive Lyceum. Its primary aim was to develop the physical, intellectual, moral and spiritual faculties of the young – the long-term objective being the promotion of: Truth, Justice, Fraternal Love, Purity, Beauty, Music, Art, Health, Science, Philosophy and Spirituality.

CHAPTER SEVEN

The Fox Sisters

Margaret Fox (1833-1893)
Kate Fox (1837- 1892)

The Fox Sisters played an important part in the emergence of what we now call modern-day Spiritualism.

Hydesville Day

Spiritualists around the world celebrate 31 March because it is classed as a day of historical importance. It is called Hydesville Day: the day representing the emergence of modern-day Spiritualism.

So, how did this come to be?

Most Spiritualists are aware that Hydesville Day has something to do with when the Fox Sisters and their parents moved to a small wooden house in the village of Hydesville, near Newark, New York State in 1847. What most people don't know, is that some of the truths surrounding their story have been distorted, but if we go back to the many statements given by neighbours who witnessed the events there, we can understand how some myths emerged from extraordinary facts.

Mrs Fox, the sisters' mother, was said to have been gifted with 'second sight'. Margaret and Kate were the sisters' names. Reports differ regarding their ages at this time. Some say Margaret was twelve, others say she was nearly fifteen; and some say Kate was nine, others say she was twelve.

Over the years, Margaret and Kate have become integral to events. However, some of the statements taken from witnesses, reveal the presence of a third girl in the household – possibly a niece. Before we go any further, we should recognise the story actually begins five years before the Fox Family moved in.

To begin with, a certain Mr and Mrs Bell resided there with their maid, Lucretia, from 1843 to 1844. One afternoon, an unnamed pedlar, allegedly an old acquaintance of the Bells, called at the house. He was aged about thirty, and was carrying a pack of material for sale. Lucretia wished to purchase some of the material, but because she had no money, she asked the pedlar to deliver it to her father's house, so he could pay the pedlar. The material, however, was never delivered, and it was not long after this that Mrs Bell, quite unexpectedly, informed Lucretia that financial constraints now meant Lucretia's services were no longer required. Lucretia moved out, only to be called back three days later to take up her original position. This was all very strange, and stranger still were the events that were about to take place.

Lucretia began to be disturbed by bizarre rapping noises in the bedroom, followed by the sound of footsteps, making their way from the bedroom to the pantry and then down into the cellar. Then one day, Mrs Bell sent Lucretia into the cellar to shut the outside door. As Lucretia made her way down and walked across the floor, she fell across a very uneven surface. It was as if she'd fallen into a hole covered with soft soil. She observed several more such holes, and asked Mrs Bell what they were. Mrs Bell told her they were rat holes, an explanation Lucretia accepted.

Noises continued. A few months later, the Bells moved out, and a Mr and Mrs Weekman moved in, only to move back out again in 1847 because of the same noises and the sighting of an apparition. It was then that the Fox Family moved in. The family knew nothing about the disturbances before moving, until very soon after arriving, they became bombarded with raps and knocking sounds. These gradually became less intense, but could still be heard at night in one of the bedrooms and sometimes coming from the cellar. The knocking then became more distinct. It would start in one part of the house, and quickly move to another. Strangely, although the sound could be relatively quiet, it created noticeable vibrations.

Then events intensified. The bedclothes were being drawn back from the girls as they slept. Objects were appearing and cold hands were touching their faces. By February 1848 the noises had become so loud they kept the family awake. In late March 1848, matters grew worse until there came the night of reckoning. Friday, 31 March 1848 arrived: the anniversary of the advent of worldwide modern-day Spiritualism.

The Fox Family were awakened by the sound of loud rapping. The neighbours were summoned to witness what was going on. Kate and Margaret began to interact with the unseen force.

They clicked their fingers and clapped their hands, and the energy responded accordingly with the correct number of raps. This frightened them, so Mrs Fox stepped in, joined by a former tenant of the house, a Mr William Deusler. Interestingly, it was Mr Deusler who devised the alphabet code that revealed certain interesting facts.

1. The invisible force was a spirit.
2. The spirit was that of a man, who had been murdered and robbed by Mr Bell.
3. Prior to the incident, the murdered man had been carrying a trunk of goods for sale.
4. The murder had taken place on a Tuesday night, at about midnight.
5. It was possible the body had been buried in the cellar.

It was eventually established that the murdered man was the pedlar who had visited the Bells to sell his goods. It has been widely reported that the pedlar's name was Charles B. Rosna, but there is no conclusive proof of this, not even with Mr Deusler's alphabet code.

Mr Fox decided to dig the floor in the cellar. Unfortunately, the house was built near a stream, so when he dug three feet down, the cellar flooded. By the summer of 1848, the land had dried sufficiently for Mr Fox to try again. This time he found bits of hair and bones, including what appeared to be a portion of skull. But that was as far as he got. Sceptics claimed that the hair and bones belonged to animals.

As far as Margaret and Kate were concerned, this was the start of the development of their mediumship. In 1849 both girls demonstrated in the Corinthian Halls in Rochester (USA). This was preceded by an investigation to see whether the girls were making the rapping sounds by cracking their joints. They passed every test. Horace Greeley, founder and editor of the *New York Tribune*, decided to look further into the matter. He sent a reporter, Charles Partridge, to investigate. Partridge concluded that the girls were authentic. Greely then arranged for them to come to New York City, where the scientific community got involved. By this time, he was well impressed with the work of the girls and their physical mediumship.

Physical Mediumship

This developed predominantly with Kate, and consisted of the appearance of materialised hands, direct writing, automatic writing and raps. The eminent chemist and physicist, Professor William Crookes, took a particular interest in her. During one of his experiments, a luminous hand materialised and descended from the upper part of the room. It began to scribble on a piece of paper, which was already in the room. There was no human contact. This was an example of direct writing (or, independent writing), which is produced purely by Spirit. Indeed, it could not have been Kate's hand, because Crookes held both her hands, and had his feet placed on her feet. The only others present in the room were his wife and a female relative. There were also reports of physical items being carried around by a materialised hand. Loved ones and departed friends were materialising. So, what was happening?

Ectoplasm and the Spirit World

Ectoplasm is etheric energy matter formed outside our physical bodies, and is a combination of dynamic energy, chemicals and physical matter. It can manifest in different forms and can create an exact physical replica of how a spirit might have looked when in their physical body. Some materialised bodies can look as solid as a physical body. It would probably be the method used in the case of Kate Fox, when a hand materialised for independent writing (direct writing).

Automatic writing

Kate Fox not only produced examples of independent writing, she also developed the skill of automatic writing where Spirit uses the arm and hand of the medium to produce a written text. But it didn't end there. What was the cause of the rapping sounds, and why were things moving all over the place?

Ectoplasmic rods

Raps can be caused by a protrusion from the medium's body of a long rod made of ectoplasm. The medium is the main source, but regular sitters will exude a certain amount of ectoplasm. The Spirit World can 'collect' physical ectoplasm and mix it with chemicals on their side. In so doing, they create a refined type of ectoplasm, which can be hardened and moulded into an ectoplasmic rod. Invisible bands (rods) of ectoplasm, coming from the body of the medium, become conductors of force, similar to electrical wires. They are not the force itself, but connect up with the object to be manipulated, like plugging in an electrical appliance.

This rod can either move physical objects, or produce the sound of rapping and knocking. Sometimes a sound like splintering, or cracking wood, can be heard. Raps or knocks are a common type of physical phenomena. The sound can be gentle or loud. The rods are invisible to the human eye (in most cases), but conduct enough energy to make sounds and strike blows. The energy force can raise an object, and even play an instrument. These rods could have been used to cause vibrations, and remove the bedclothes from the Fox Sisters' beds as they slept. They could also have been used to carry books and other objects.

Levitation of objects: psychokinetic energy (telekinesis / PK)

This is the ability to move an object without coming into physical contact with it. It is the psychic ability to use the power of the mind to manipulate a specific target, and make it do what you want. There have been cases where the process has been applied unwittingly by pubescent girls and boys, and it may have played a part in some of the activities surrounding the Fox Sisters.

What is deemed to be 'poltergeist activity' (unexplained disturbances such as loud noises and disruptive movement of objects) could actually be down to all, or some of the energy of the child. What is clear in the case of the Fox Sisters, is that the pedlar played a very significant part.

What happened to Margaret and Kate?

The Spirit World, like the physical world, is comprised of different kinds of energies, which must be worked with wisely. It is, therefore, important that mediums work in truth, light and love, and ask that only those from the highest realms come forward. Neither Margaret, nor Kate, were given the chance to appreciate the moral implications of Spiritualism. Unscrupulous and devious individuals were plying them with alcohol, in the belief they would 'perform' better. They were placed under tremendous pressure and, sadly, became alcohol dependent.

In 1857 Margaret married Dr Elisha Kane, the Arctic explorer. Dr Kane, worried by the alcohol use, tried to draw both Margaret and Kate away from Spiritualism. When he died soon after the marriage, Margaret decided to abandon Spiritualism, and turned to the Roman Catholic Church.

In 1871, Kate toured England to spread the word of Spiritualism. A year later, she married a London barrister (Mr H. D. Jencken) who was also a Spiritualist. During the late 1880s, J. J. Morse (well-known nineteenth-century trance medium) brought Kate over from America to the Glasgow Association of Spiritualists, where she demonstrated her mediumship.

Unfortunately, as the years progressed, matters took a turn for the worse. Both sisters had become very heavy drinkers, and many opponents of Spiritualism jumped upon their alcohol use in a bid to discredit them.

Margaret had become very unstable. When she and Kate were given the financial incentive to denounce everything they had done, they did exactly that, only to eventually acknowledge that their renunciation of Spiritualism had, in fact, been a lie.

And herein lies the truth of the matter. We are all human. We are all vulnerable, some of us more than others. We have choice, but circumstances very often influence our choices. We don't always make the right decisions, but we certainly learn from our mistakes. Human life is one big lesson. We are here to work with what we are given. Our mistakes of the past, as painful as they might be, are a steppingstone to a new path; a path of experience, knowledge and better understanding.

Celebrating Hydesville Day

It is important to remember when reviewing the emergence of modern-day Spiritualism, we should consider not only the parts played by the Fox Sisters, but by the entire Fox Family and all their neighbours. Each was a visionary, in their own way. Every one of those present was determined to get to the truth. It was a truth uncovered fifty years later by chance when, in 1904, children found a human skeleton behind a crumbling wall in the Hydesville cellar. *The Boston Journal* reported in an article dated 23 November 1904 that a doctor had been consulted, and that he concluded that the bones were human and approximately fifty years old, thus fitting in with the timeline of the murder.

CHAPTER EIGHT

Robert Owen

(1771-1858)

Robert Owen was a Welsh textile manufacturer and social reformer. He would also become instrumental in the emergence of modern-day Spiritualism.

Early Life

Owen strongly believed that human character evolves from circumstances, but it was not until late on in his life that he became a Spiritualist. His father was a saddler, ironmonger and the local postmaster. His mother came from a Newtown farming family. He received little formal education, but was an avid reader. He left school aged ten, and entered the drapery business, becoming apprentice to a draper for four years.

Owen the Businessman

Over the years, Owen developed skills in business and management. He also had a particular interest in improving working conditions for factory workers, and would later become one of the founders of Utopian Socialism and the Cooperative Movement. In 1799, he married Ann Caroline Dale, the daughter of David Dale, who was a Glasgow philanthropist, and proprietor of the New Lanark Mills, which was a large textile mill. In the summer of 1799, Owen and his partners bought the New Lanark Mills from David Dale, and turned them into the New Lanark Village, which is now a world heritage site.

Two thousand individuals were associated with the Mill – five hundred of them children, brought there, at the age of five or six, from the poorhouses and charities of Edinburgh and Glasgow. Owen became an avid supporter of youth education and early childcare, and was the founder of nursery schools.

Owen strove to improve not only factory conditions, but the lives of the workers. His social and economic ideas at the Mill proved successful. He won the confidence of the workers, and earned an international reputation. In 1813 he wrote *A New View of Society, or Essays on the Principle of the Formation of the Human Character.* He concluded that good character can only result by placing individuals under proper environmental influences (physical, moral and social), as early as possible. In 1818, he opened the Institute for the Formation of Character at New Lanark. This, together with other educational programmes, provided free education from infancy to adulthood.

In 1825, he decided to test the viability of self-sufficient working communities. He experimented with communal living in America: the most famous community being New Harmony, Indiana. It was an ambitious effort, and was his preliminary model for a utopian community. With the assistance of a new financial partner, William Maclure, a wealthy Scottish scientist and philanthropist living in Philadelphia, Owen was able to attract scientists, educators and artists, and these individuals helped to establish the utopian community at New Harmony as a centre for educational reform, scientific research, and artistic expression. When Owen returned to Britain to continue his work, he left New Harmony under the supervision of his two sons, Robert Dale Owen and William Owen. Unfortunately, the project proved to be an economic failure and New Harmony was dissolved in 1827.

Spiritualism

In 1817, Owen had declared that all religions were false. In 1854, he had a series of sittings with Maria B Haydon, an American medium, following which, he converted to Spiritualism. He was eighty-three years of age. After his conversion, Owen claimed to have had mediumistic contact with the spirits of Benjamin Franklin (a founding father of the United States) and Thomas Jefferson (third president of the United States). He believed the purpose of these communications was to render the world a more spiritual place.

On 17 November 1858, Owen died in his native village of Newton in Wales.

CHAPTER NINE

Emma Hardinge Britten

(1823-1899)

The Philosophy of Spiritualism is based on information that was passed on by the spirit of Robert Owen through the trance mediumship of Emma Hardinge Britten, who became one of the main pioneers in spreading the word of Spiritualism.

Early Life

Emma was born in the East End of London. As a child, she was able to predict future events and would often see the spirits of relatives and family friends. When her father died in 1834, she began working as a musician and opera singer. She joined a secret London occult society, which experimented with clairvoyance. In 1855 Emma went to America for the first time. Whilst there she visited a medium, who highlighted her mediumistic abilities, and told her that Spirit would make itself known to her through table tilting and rapping. In 1856, Emma held a table séance where a message was spelled out from a friend, who had just died on a ship that had sunk. No one knew of this prior to the séance.

Emma became a popular medium in America, and often worked alongside other mediums like Kate Fox. Emma's mediumistic gifts included automatic and inspirational writing, inspirational addresses, psychometry (sensing or reading the history of an object by touching it) and healing. But this was not enough for Emma. She gave up platform mediumship to concentrate on inspirational speaking.

Theosophy

Emma travelled throughout America and many other parts of the world to give lectures and inspired addresses on the subject of Modern Spiritualism. Her public speaking and prolific writing helped encourage the formation of many spiritualist groups, societies and churches throughout the world. In 1875, Emma was among the founders of the Theosophical Society in New York, which was set up to promote Theosophy. Theosophy is based upon older European and Asian religions and draws its beliefs, predominantly, from the writings of Helena Blavatsky, who was a Russian immigrant, and principal founder of the Society. It was set up to promote values of universal brotherhood and social improvement, but without stipulating particular ethical codes. Emma did not agree with everything it believed in, and soon severed her connections with Madame Blavatsky.

Returning to Britain

Emma returned to Britain, and in 1887, she founded the magazine: *Two Worlds*, which she edited for the next five years. Between 1892 and 1893 she was editor of the British publication: *The Unseen Universe*. Although she would not live to see it, her dream of establishing a proper and formal 'school of prophets' (training school for mediums) came to fruition in 1900, with the founding of the Britten Memorial Institute and Library in Manchester. Emma proved herself to be one of the main pioneers in spreading the word of Spiritualism. She worked exhaustively, helping to shape Spiritualism into what it is today.

So, what is SNU Spiritualism?

The SNU is the Spiritualists' National Union. Spiritualism is an officially recognised religious movement with its own churches, ministers, officiants and volunteers who possess the same rights and privileges as other religions. It has no fixed creed or dogma, but embodies the main ideas of all religions – in particular, that there is life after death.

Its use of mediumship can offer evidence, which for some people is enough proof to them that their loved one has survived physical death.

The SNU's principles are based on information delivered by the spirit of Robert Owen (see previous chapter) and other communicators. Mrs Britten used this information to compile: *The Ten Spiritual Commandments* and *The Ten Laws of Right*, which have been moulded into the Seven Principles of Spiritualism:

1. The Fatherhood of God.
2. The Brotherhood of Man.
3. The Communion of Spirits and the Ministry of Angels.
4. The Continuous Existence of the Human Soul.
5. Personal Responsibility.
6. Compensation and Retribution Hereafter for all the Good and Evil Deeds done on Earth.
7. Eternal Progress Open to every Human Soul.

What is a Medium?

Mediums are ordinary people who have, through training, developed their natural psychic ability to enable them to reach out and communicate with those in the Spirit World. There are three types of mediumship: physical, mental and spiritual healing.

Physical Mediumship

Examples of this would be materialisation or levitation of objects witnessed by more than one person. Another example would be direct voice, where spirit speaks through the medium's voice box, or independently, through a spirit-made voice box, and where the sound or words emitted can be heard by more than one person.

Mental Mediumship

This is: clairvoyance (seeing spirit), clairaudience (hearing spirit) and clairsentience (sensing spirit), perceived only by the medium.

Spiritual Healing

Spiritual healing is the channelling of healing energies from the Spirit World through a healer to a patient, and is based on the reality of a divine universal energy which exists in all things. Spiritual healing is not limited to humans. Wherever there is life there can be a transference of energy for healing.

Healing at Glasgow Association of Spiritualists

Spiritual healing is practised at Glasgow Association of Spiritualists by fully-qualified and licensed SNU healers. Although they cannot guarantee a complete cure, they can alleviate suffering and ease a passing.

Contact Healing: Contact healing is when the healing medium seeks permission to place their hands on to the patient during healing.

Absent Healing: In absent healing the patient is not physically present and healing thoughts are extended to them.

Distant Healing: Distant healing is healing sent by the power of thought to someone who is physically present but is not receiving contact healing.

Patients generally find that healing is a pleasant, relaxing and gratifying experience. Sometimes they become hot, or cold, or, can feel a slight tingling sensation. Pain can be dispersed, or, diminished. The healer will link with the Spirit World on behalf of the patient, and the blending of energies allows the healing process to begin. There are no side-effects to this therapy, which is completely natural. It is not offered as an alternative to orthodox medicine – it is complementary. Spiritual healing is very much a holistic discipline, with the implicit belief that health is not simply a matter of being free of symptoms of disease, but of the harmony of the whole person at all levels – spiritual, emotional, physical and mental.

CHAPTER TEN

Davenport Brothers

Ira Erastus Davenport (1839-1911)
William Henry Davenport (1841-1877)

The Davenport Brothers produced excellent examples of physical mediumship.

Early Life

The Davenport Brothers were born in Buffalo in the State of New York. Their family were early English settlers in America. Life in the Davenport household was not without incident. Raps, thumps, loud noises, snaps and crackling noises were all regular sounds, but it was not until they heard about the Fox Sisters, that they decided to investigate what exactly was going on. The boys would sit with their sister, Elizabeth, and experiment by placing their hands on a table. Loud and violent noises could be heard, and as happened with the Fox Sisters, messages could be spelled out.

Physical Phenomena

When the brothers were young, they produced many different types of physical phenomena. Ira Davenport developed the skill of automatic writing, where Spirit used his arm and hand to produce a written text. He regularly produced information he could not possibly have known.

On one occasion, a pencil was seen to write in broad daylight. There was no human contact. This was an example of direct writing (or, independent writing), produced purely by Spirit.

As with the Fox Sisters, ectoplasmic rods enabled Ira to levitate in the air above the heads of those in a room. Quite often he was nine feet from the floor. Over time, William and Elizabeth were able to do the same thing. At times, kitchen utensils would dance around the table and float in the air when the family were at breakfast, and during séances, musical instruments were reported to float and play above the sitters' heads.

During tests and public séances, the brothers would be tied down with ropes. When it was felt this was not enough, the professors of Harvard University would handcuff them and hold them down. They would then be placed in a cabinet, one of the professors sitting between them. But still the Spirit World intervened. Lights appeared, as did ectoplasmic hands; instruments would be rattled above the head of the professor sitting between them, and unseen spirit operators would untie the brothers, and place the ropes round the professor's head.

Further developments

When the boys were in their twenties, they travelled to England. They were keen to prove to the intellectual and scientific classes that there are intelligent forces, or powerful intelligences, beyond the range of 'normal' philosophy. They wanted to show that a new universe could be opened to human thought and investigation.

In London, leading scientists of the day and newspaper reporters attended private séances. The *Morning Post* reported that those present were told to make a critical examination to ensure that no fraud took place. Physical phenomena were reported, and no fraud detected.

CHAPTER ELEVEN

Eddy Brothers

William Eddy (1838-1932)
Horatio Eddy (1842-1922)

The Eddy Brothers also produced examples of physical mediumship.

Early Life

The Eddy Brothers were farmers from Vermont in the USA. From an early age, they were able to produce physical phenomena, consisting of rapping, movement of objects and levitation. It was claimed that their great-great-great-great grandmother had been tried as a witch during the Salem trials in 1692, but had managed to escape.

Their mother, Julia, came from a long line of mediums and psychics, but their father, Zephaniah, hated what they were doing, and physically abused them. Life was, therefore, hard for the young Eddy boys, but as they got older, Zephaniah changed tactics. He realised he could make money out of their abilities, so forced them into doing what they had always been able to do.

To show that the brothers were not interfering, and that the phenomena were genuine, they were usually tied up with ropes (sealed with burning wax), and their hands were secured with handcuffs.

Colonel Henry Steel Olcott

During the latter part of August, 1874, Colonel Henry Steel Olcott was sent by the *New York Sun* to investigate the brothers. Colonel Olcott was an American military officer, journalist, lawyer and co-founder (with Helena Blavatsky and Emma Hardinge Britten) of the Theosophical Society. He stayed on their farm for five days, returning a short time later, this time as special correspondent for the *Daily Graphic*, where he took up residence for two and a half months. During this time, he made detailed notes of all the phenomena he witnessed, and compiled fifteen articles, which appeared consecutively in the *Daily Graphic* in October and November 1874. These caused a sensation throughout America and Europe.

Olcott expressed his absolute confidence in the psychic abilities of the brothers. He was witness to various examples of mediumship (mental and physical), which included: automatic writing, psychometry, materialisation, direct voice and healing.

Cabinets and materialisation

Olcott described his experiences with the Eddy Brothers in his book: *People from the Other World*. He also explained that cabinets were used for materialisation because the ectoplasmic vapour could be more easily condensed in a limited space. He added that the mediums did not have to be in the cabinet. They could be next to it, although the materialised forms always emerged from within the cabinet.

Apparitions

Olcott observed around four hundred apparitions emerging from the cabinet over a twelve-week period. He noted figures of different sizes, races and sexes: Native American Indians (some smoking tobacco), babes in arms, gentlemen in evening dress and ladies in fine costumes.

How were these figures formed?

Olcott looked at the properties of ectoplasm. Because it is a protean substance, it has the ability to assume different forms. This means it is capable of being moulded instantly into any shape. He went on to investigate the fabric of the materialised forms, and was able to measure and weigh them. He also showed that the human body loses weight when it produces ectoplasm in the air.

Vocal communication

During séances, there would usually be one controlling spiritual being, who would organise the rest of the figures. This being might speak, or simply direct the others, and very often, it would be a Native American Indian, who in their physical life had had an affinity with spiritual phenomena.

CHAPTER TWELVE

David Duguid

(1832-1907)

David Duguid was a spirit artist, direct voice medium and spirit photographer.

Background

David Duguid was born in Dunfermline (Scotland), and began life as a cabinet-maker, but by 1866 had developed a great interest in Spiritualism.

Mediumship

Duguid began by attending table-tilting séances. Gradually his own skills in mediumship developed, until he became a gifted physical medium. Like the Fox Sisters, he was able to produce rapping sounds, make objects move, and cause musical boxes to sail around the séance room, and at times, he himself, was levitated.

Spirit Artist

Duguid was also a spirit artist. This meant that when he was in trance, the Spirit World could control his hand, allowing him to draw and paint. There were also instances when Spirit would materialise and paint on to the canvas whilst his hands were restrained.

His drawings began as rough sketches of flowers and vases, but the spirit controls complained that they could not properly express themselves because of Duguid's own lack of artistic skills. The controls suggested that Duguid take art classes, which he did for four months at the Government School of Arts. These classes greatly assisted Duguid, and the Spirit World was now able to make use of him to produce intricate and detailed works, many of them painted on small card.

Controls

Duguid's first control was a spirit called Marcus Baker, an artist from Belgium (date of birth and date of death unknown). This spirit allowed Duguid to reproduce a known masterpiece: *The Waterfall*, by Jacob Ruisdael (Dutch artist, c 1629 – 1682).

Hafed Prince of Persia

Between 1870 and 1871, Duguid sat in trance for forty-six sittings, during which time, a spirit named Hafed came through and dictated a history of his life. Hafed had lived nineteen hundred years before, and had been a Persian warrior prince. He had travelled extensively, and was able to give an account of life in ancient Persia, Greece, Egypt, Judaea and Babylon.

(*See Hafed, Prince of Persia by Hay Nisbet; and Hermes, a Disciple of Jesus: His Life and Missionary Work; Also, the Evangelistic Travels of Anah and Zitha, together with Incidents in the Life of Jesus, Spirit Communications Received Through D. Duguid, by Hay Nisbet.*)

Direct Voice

David Duguid was also a direct voice medium. He was able to channel voices from the Spirit World which ranged from a whisper to a loud thunderous tone.

Spirit Photography

Duguid went on to apply his mediumship to spirit photography. He took many photos where images of spirit entities were captured.

James Robertson and Andrew Glendinning of the Glasgow Association of Spiritualists, who were also investigators of spirit photography, had already developed a number of explanations for similar such images produced in other cases, labelling them either fraud, psychic or spirit-based. They went on to study Duguid's images, as did Professor James Coates (past secretary of the Glasgow Association of Spiritualists), and believed that they were spirit-based.

Spirit Photography: Dr John Winning

As spirit photography continued to develop, Dr John Winning (Lyceum Conductor at the Glasgow Association of Spiritualists from 1940-1965), took a special interest in it. He was associated with the Society for the Study of Supernatural Pictures, which was a psychical research organisation established in 1918 in London, to promote the scientific study and investigation of supernormal pictures. Not only did Dr Winning take photographs with 'spirit extras', he had his own circle, which produced great examples of materialisation, also captured on camera.

CHAPTER THIRTEEN

Daniel Dunglas Home

(1833-1886)

Daniel Dunglas Home was a healer and medium.

Background

Daniel Dunglas Home was born in Currie, near Edinburgh. There is some mystery about his parentage, and a possibility he was related to the family of the Earl of Home. At the age of nine, Daniel was adopted by an aunt and moved with her to New England (America). By the age of thirteen, he was showing signs of psychic ability: something his aunt did not appreciate. When Daniel told his aunt he had foreseen the death of his friend, Edwin, and the death of his mother, she turned him out, believing he had brought the 'devil' into her house, forcing him to move around and stay with different people. Notwithstanding, his mediumship developed. He held up to six or seven séances a day, and people flocked to see him. He also had extraordinary healing powers and began to study for the medical profession, until illness forced him to give this up. Hard work was taking its toll on his health, and his left lung was damaged. Finally, following medical advice, he returned to Britain and ended up living in Liverpool.

Honesty and mission to demonstrate immortality

Daniel was known as D. D. Home. He was a very honest person. Throughout his career as a medium, he never sought payment. His relationship with mediumship, however, lacked consistency. It would leave him for months, then return, stronger than ever.

Psychical Research

Many eminent professors and professionals supported D. D. Home, and became Spiritualists. These included Judge John Worth Edmonds of the New York Supreme Court. D. D. Home also demonstrated his skills many times in the presence of scientists, including Professor William Crookes and Sir David Brewster. Both scientists attended séances with him, where the sitters would sit at a moderately-sized table.

On one occasion, Brewster said that when the table moved, an incredible sensation ran up his arms. The table then rose from the floor on its own. Brewster also commented that when a small hand bell was laid on the floor, it rang on its own, before actually coming over to him and placing itself in his hand. He could find no mechanical means that would cause this to happen.

D. D. Home also demonstrated his physical mediumship in the presence of royalty, notably, Napoleon III, the Emperor of Russia, Emperor William I of Germany and various kings of Bavaria and Wurttemberg. But it was his ability to levitate that proved significant.

Levitation

D. D. Home was seen by many reliable witnesses to float in the air whilst in trance. This happened many times. On one occasion he was seen in a chateau in Bordeaux to float to the ceiling. On another, he rose from a chair, about five feet above the ground. His figure then passed from one side of the window to the other, feet foremost, whilst he was lying horizontally. This was witnessed by medical professionals.

On another occasion, D. D. Home was raised from the ground, until his hand touched the top of a door. He then floated forward, horizontally. Another time, his face transfigured and shone, following which, he rose twice to the ceiling, leaving the mark of a pencilled cross on the ceiling to assure witnesses they were not hallucinating.

Private life

In 1858 D. D. Home married Alexandria de Kroll, the 17-year-old daughter of a noble Russian family, in Saint Petersburg. Interestingly, his Best Man was Alexandre Dumas, French writer and author of *The Count of Monte Cristo* and *The Three Musketeers*. The couple had a son, Gregoire, but Alexandria fell ill with tuberculosis, and died in 1862. In October 1871, D. D. Home married Julie de Gloumeline, a wealthy Russian, whom he also met in St Petersburg. He eventually converted to the Greek Orthodox faith.

Death

D. D. Home suffered from tuberculosis for most of his life, and as the disease advanced, it affected his mediumistic skills. Eventually, he was forced to retire. He died in 1886, aged fifty-three, and was buried in the Russian cemetery of St Germain-en-Laye in Paris.

CHAPTER FOURTEEN

Reverend William Stainton Moses

(1839-1892)

William Stainton Moses was a minister of the Church of England, Spiritualist and medium.

Early life

Stainton Moses was born in Donington near Lincoln (England) and educated at Bedford School, followed by University College School, London and Exeter College, Oxford. In 1870, he was ordained as a minister of the Church of England by Bishop Samuel Wilberforce, and carried out his duties, first on the Isle of Man, then in Dorset.

Introduction to Spiritualism

Unfortunately, ill-health forced Stainton Moses to cease his clerical duties. He moved to London to take up a teaching post at University College School (until 1889). He also took on a private teaching post. His pupil was the son of a Dr Stanhope Templeman Speer and his wife, who were Spiritualists, and it was they who introduced him to Spiritualism.

Dr Speer was a British physician and mountain climber. He worked at Brompton Hospital in London, and specialised in treating chest diseases. He has been described as the first physician to describe mountain sickness in a medical journal. Dr Speer was an early member of The Ghost Club, a paranormal investigation and research organisation (still in existence today), founded in London in 1862: believed to be the oldest such organisation in the world. The Club investigated ghosts and hauntings. Notable members included Charles Dickens and Sir Arthur Conan Doyle. Dr Speer was also a member of the Society for Psychical Research, which still runs today. Its purpose is to understand events and abilities commonly described as psychic or paranormal.

Séances: physical phenomena

In 1872 Stainton Moses began to sit in circle with Dr and Mrs Speer. They would encounter different types of physical phenomena, including table rapping, levitation of objects, manifestation of apports (where the Spirit World displaces an object from the spirit vibration to the physical vibration) and fragrant odours. There were even reports of Stainton Moses being levitated. As time progressed, manifestations began to diversify. The circle witnessed examples of direct writing and automatic writing. On one occasion, a blank piece of paper was placed under the table before the séance took place. When the séance finished, the sitters found the word, 'Imperator', written on the paper. It turned out that Imperator would become Stainton Moses' famous spirit control.

Stainton Moses was able to see his control clairvoyantly. He soon learned that Imperator was in charge of a band of spirits attempting to teach the human race the fundamentals of existence through automatic writing. Direct voice also played a significant part. Voices from the Spirit World would come through the air, and speak through a spirit voice box located directly above the sitters (independent direct voice). Then there was trance voice, where the spirits used Stainton Moses' entranced body (his own larynx) to speak. Witnesses were able to say that it was always clear that the personality addressing the group was not that of the medium. The voices were different and the ideas expressed were often contrary to Stainton Moses' own views. Different spirits would come through, but Imperator was the chief communicator. Imperator explained that he was the Chief of a band of forty-nine spirits, and that it was his role to guide and direct the other spirits in their work. Imperator added that he had two spirit assistants, named 'Rector' and 'Doctor'.

When Imperator spoke through Stainton Moses, the sitters usually observed rays of light, including a large, bright cross of light behind his head. It was several feet high and moved from side to side. When one of the sitters asked what this was, Imperator explained that the pillar of light was himself, and the bright rays behind him were his attendants.

On 30 March 1873, spirit messages started coming through Stainton Moses' hand, by means of automatic writing. To begin with, the writing was very small and irregular, and he had to write slowly. However, as time progressed, the writing became more regular and more legible. Most of the early messages came from Doctor, but gradually, other spirits started using Stainton Moses' hand. Each spirit was distinguished by different handwriting and peculiarities of style and expression. When some of them found they could not influence Stainton Moses' hand, they called upon Rector for assistance.

Stainton Moses, however, was faced with a problem. Much of what the spirits were saying seemed to contradict Christian dogma and doctrine. What if Imperator and his band were really evil spirits attempting to lead both him and the human race astray? Imperator was pleased that Stainton Moses had an enquiring mind and told him that this was one of the reasons he had been chosen as their vessel.

Imperator went on to explain that there is a point, beyond which, it is impossible to provide evidence. For definite proof, Stainton Moses had to be content to wait until physical death, when he would return to the Spirit World.

Stainton Moses continually asked who Imperator, Rector and Doctor had been when they had lived their lives as physical human beings. To begin with, Imperator would not say, but eventually revealed their names – stipulating that their identities should not be exposed. After Stainton Moses' death, their identities were made public in a book by A. W. Trethewy: *The Controls of Stainton Moses.*

Imperator was Malachias (an Old Testament prophet), Rector was the Roman Christian theologian Hippolytus (170 CE – 235 CE) and Doctor was the Greek philosopher, Athenodorus (74 BCE – 7 CE), who, interestingly, was reported to have been confronted by a ghost, whilst living in a rented house in Athens. The ghost, who was bound with chains, asked Athenodorus to follow him, and led him to a courtyard, before disappearing. Athenodorus marked the spot, and the next day, with the permission of the city magistrates, he dug up the earth from that spot, where he found the skeleton of an old man, bound with chains. After the skeleton was given a proper burial, the ghost was said to have never haunted that house again. If this story is true, then the incident must, indeed, be a precursor to the case of the Fox Sisters.

CHAPTER FIFTEEN

Madame d'Esperance: aka Elizabeth Hope

(1855-1919)

Madame d'Esperance was a medium who specialised in automatic writing and materialisation and produced many apports from the Spirit World.

Early life

Madame d'Esperance was born in the East End of London. As a child, she had 'shadow friends', and could see objects, which other people could not (clairvoyance). She became a trance medium, but in addition, was able to provide good evidence of physical mediumship, including, materialisation, psychokinesis (moving objects by mental effort), apports and automatic writing. She was also a writer, and travelled extensively throughout Europe, giving séances in Denmark, France, Norway, Belgium, Sweden and Germany.

Automatic writing

As Elizabeth grew older, her skills in automatic writing developed. Information would be transmitted to her from the Spirit World, after which, she would write it down in semi-trance. The subjects addressed would depend entirely on the personality and ages of the sitters.

Apports

During one séance, a pair of cufflinks dropped out of nowhere into someone's cup of coffee. These were apports, which had crossed from the Spirit World into the physical world. Apports would usually appear when Elizabeth was in a cabinet, and when none of the sitters was actually willing it to happen. Elizabeth was the first to admit that she had no idea how it happened.

William Oxley

William Oxley, poet and psychical researcher, said that he once witnessed twenty-seven roses (apports) appearing at one of Elizabeth's séances. Another time, a rare plant (*Ixora Crocata*) appeared. He photographed it the next day, and asked his gardener to take care of it. The plant went on to live for three months.

Attempts to prove fraud

During another séance, an unnamed sitter, who was desperate to 'expose' Elizabeth as a fraud, grabbed hold of her whilst she was in deep trance. Elizabeth later described the intense fear and pain that resulted from this physical contact. She felt she was sinking into an abyss. When she finally regained consciousness, she felt very unwell, particularly in the area of her lungs.

Sir Arthur Conan Doyle

Sir Arthur Conan Doyle (physician, writer and psychical researcher) was another great supporter of Elizabeth's. At first, he was doubtful as to her authenticity, then changed his mind. He said that whilst at a séance, he had witnessed the materialisation of many different faces.

CHAPTER SIXTEEN

Florence Cook

(1856-1904)

Florence Cook was another great physical medium who underwent great scrutiny by the psychical researchers.

Early life

Florence Cook was a British medium who was aware of Spirit throughout her life; unfortunately, during her childhood years, this was put down to little more than a vivid imagination. In 1871, when she was fifteen years of age, she attended a tea party at a friend's house. She and her friends decided to experiment with table-tilting. On so doing, strange things began to happen. The table became unmanageable and Florence was unexpectedly levitated. Her mother, who was present during these strange occurrences, fast realised that Florence did not simply have a vivid imagination; she had been telling the truth. It became abundantly clear that the Spirit World was trying to make used of Florence's mediumistic skills.

Florence and her mother began sessions together at home. During one of the sittings, Florence engaged in 'mirror image' automatic writing. Her mediumistic skills developed. She sat in public séances with other physical mediums, until her mother intervened, and insisted that séances should be held in private. It was then that the spirit of Katie King stepped in. Katie was the daughter of John King: alias, Captain Henry Owen Morgan, Welsh buccaneer and pirate. During the quiet sessions with her mother, Florence would go into trance, and Katie would come forward, promising to reveal many strange things.

Poltergeist Activity

Unfortunately, things began to get out of hand. Florence was still only fifteen years of age, but worked at one of the schools as a teacher. When poltergeist-type activities began to occur whenever she was present, Florence was forced to leave.

Hackney Circle

Not to be discouraged, Florence and her parents formed the Hackney Circle. This was comprised of Florence, her parents, sisters (also mediums) and the family maid (Mary). The circle became famous, and when it came to the notice of Mr Charles Blackburn (a wealthy citizen of Manchester), Florence was guaranteed an annual retaining fee if she ensured she would be free to give her services when required. Financially secure, the Hackney Circle thrived. It encouraged a lively and happy atmosphere.

The spirit of Katie King appeared on many occasions, and as time went on, she was able to show herself more clearly. Her materialisation began as a face, which was hollow at the back, but later filled out.

A year later, Katie's spirit was able to walk out the cabinet. A short time later, she stood and posed for flashlight photography. But this created another problem: the resemblance to Florence did not go unnoticed. It was time for scientific intervention.

Sir William Crookes

Sir William Crookes was preeminent in the world of science, and in 1872, he was tasked with proving the integrity of Florence Cook. His findings proved positive, and in April 1874, he wrote an article in *The Spiritualist,* describing how the materialised form of Katie walked around the room for nearly two hours, during which time, she conversed with the sitters. Clearly, as far as he was concerned, Florence Cook was 'the real deal'.

CHAPTER SEVENTEEN

Leonora Piper

(1859-1950)

Leonora Piper was a famous American medium, who specialised in direct voice and automatic writing.

Early Life

Mrs Piper was the subject of intense interest and investigation by American and British psychical research associations. She discovered her mediumistic abilities in 1884 at the time she was diagnosed with a tumour. She sat with a blind healing medium, and during the second sitting, lost consciousness and became controlled by the spirit of a young Indian girl, who called herself 'Chlorine'.

Chlorine was then replaced by the spirit of Dr Jean Phinuit Sclivellee, a Frenchman – known simply as Dr Phinuit. During trance sessions, Dr Phinuit used direct voice to explain that he had died around 1860, when aged seventy years. Phinuit would often introduce other spirits, who would give lectures about matters way beyond the comprehension of Mrs Piper.

On 6 September 1888, an artist (J. Rogers Rich) had a sitting with her. Mr Rich observed a remarkable change in Mrs Piper's voice as it became unmistakably male, and somewhat husky. The voice spoke in French, so Mr Rich responded in French. It went on to advise Mr Rich of herbal treatments to alleviate particular physical ailments, so it was assumed that this was Dr Phinuit. At further sessions, Phinuit went on to relay correct information using the alphabet: in French.

The Psychical Researchers get involved

Mrs Piper, like many other mediums of her time, was investigated by Sir Oliver Lodge (British physicist and writer), Richard Hodgson (researcher and parapsychologist: someone who studies the evidence for psychic phenomena and other paranormal activities) and James H. Hyslop (professor of ethics and logic, psychologist, and psychical researcher). On 21 December 1889, Dr Phinuit came through, and said to Sir Oliver: *'Edmund sends his love'*. Phinuit was referring to Edmund Gurney (psychologist and parapsychologist), who had died in 1888. This was significant because Gurney had founded the Society for Psychical Research in 1882, together with Frederic Myers (poet, classicist and philologist), William Barrett (physicist and parapsychologist) and Henry Sidgwick (philosopher and economist).

Sir Oliver went on to question Gurney about Dr Phinuit and Mrs Piper, and the response was that Mrs Piper was a true medium, but he had his doubts where Phinuit was concerned. Gurney described Phinuit as good hearted, but eccentric. He also found him very vulgar.

George Pelham: automatic writing

In 1892, Dr Phinuit began to turn his primary control function over to a spirit named, George Pelham. Pelham's role was to guide Mrs Piper's hand and help her to develop skills in automatic writing. During the 'handover' period there are records showing that whilst entranced, Mrs Piper would be writing something (under the guidance of Pelham) about one subject, whilst, at the same time, Dr Phinuit would be relaying completely different information from different spirits using direct voice. This continued for some time – Pelham the primary control, Dr Phinuit, the secondary.

Rector of the Imperator Band of 49

Over time, Dr Phinuit and Pelham were both replaced by Rector of the Imperator Band of 49. Rector had earlier controlled the Reverend William Stainton Moses and was later identified as the Roman Christian theologian Hippolytus (170 CE – 235 CE). Rector advised the researchers that Mrs Piper's health was weakening, and she needed rest and better management. He expressed his concerns about the continued involvement of Dr Phinuit. Phinuit made his last appearance on 26 January 1896.

Verdicts

Mrs Piper's work was of tremendous importance. For several decades her powers were tested to such a high degree that Psychical Research now owes an enormous debt to her generous and sustained cooperation, often under difficult circumstances. When James H. Hyslop wrote an article about her in the *Psychological Review*, he said that Mrs Piper's authenticity could not be doubted. For fifteen years, she had been under very close scrutiny, during which time, nothing suspicious had ever been observed.

CHAPTER EIGHTEEN

Reverend George Vale Owen

(1869-1931)

George Vale Owen was a vicar and medium, who specialised in automatic writing.

Background

George Vale Owen was born in Birmingham, and educated at the Midland Institute. In 1893, he was ordained by the Bishop of Liverpool as curate in the parish of Seaforth. He then became curate at Fairfield. This was followed by St Matthew's (Liverpool). In 1900 he became a vicar and moved to a church in Orford, Warrington, but when his mother died in 1909, strange things began to happen. It soon became clear that his psychic abilities were awakening.

Spiritualism

Owen's wife developed the power of automatic writing. Through her writing, Owen learned that he was to sit quietly with a pencil and write down any thoughts that were projected into his mind. At first, sentences appeared to make no sense, as they jumped from one subject to another. With practice, however, the sentences took on a better form, and by 1913, he was receiving clear messages. This impacted on him so much, he converted to Spiritualism; but it incurred the disapproval of the Bishop. During the 1920s, he incorporated the messages into books, the most notable being the five-volume set: *Life Beyond the Veil*.

Support and recognition

The volumes were prefaced by the well-known writer, Sir Arthur Conan Doyle, who was one of Owen's greatest supporters, but Conan Doyle was not alone in the support. Lord Northcliffe, otherwise known as Alfred Charles William Harmsworth, 1st Viscount Northcliffe, was a British newspaper and publishing magnate. As owner of the *Daily Mail* and the *Daily Mirror*, he was an early developer of popular journalism, and the foremost newspaper proprietor of the day. He exercised vast influence over British popular opinion during the Edwardian era, and published summaries of Owen's work in his journal: *The Weekly Dispatch*. Northcliffe said that he was impressed by the great sincerity and unshakeable conviction of Owen, and that he clearly possessed great spiritual gifts. Unfortunately, the church authorities were not impressed. They forced Owen out of his parish. This had a severe impact on him, including the loss of his primary source of income.

In 1922, aged fifty-three, Owen began actively promoting Spiritualism. He went on a lecture tour to the United States. This was followed by more than one hundred and fifty lectures in England. Owen eventually became pastor of a Spiritualist church in London. His financial resources, however, became severely depleted because he knew that if he received any money from his efforts, he would be accused of falsely creating messages from the Spirit World just for the purpose of profit. To help him, Conan Doyle organised a collection. This resulted in a trust fund that provided financial support for Owen during the rest of his life.

CHAPTER NINETEEN

John Campbell Sloan

(1869-1951)

John Campbell Sloan was a trance and mental medium from Glasgow. His early experiences of psychic/spiritual phenomena began when he was just a boy. He was closely examined by the psychical researcher, Arthur Findlay.

Mediumship

John worked as a shopkeeper and packer in a warehouse. These jobs served to finance himself and his family, because he refused to accept any form of financial remuneration for his services as a medium. His mediumship included trance and telekinesis (the ability to move objects at a distance by mental power). Materialisation, direct voice, clairvoyance, clairaudience and apports were also common features of his mediumship. He never used a cabinet for his work, as did most other mediums when working with physical phenomena. John's spirit guide was named 'White Feather', an American Native Indian, whom he liked to refer to as: 'Whitie'. Whitie would speak through John, using direct voice.

Research by Arthur Findlay

Arthur Findlay was a psychical researcher, who later bequeathed Stansted Hall to the Spiritualists' National Union for the advancement of Psychic Science. In 1918 he attended one of John's séances in a Spiritualist church in Glasgow. At first, Findlay was very sceptical, but when the séance continued for three hours, during the course of which, thirty separate voices spoke, each in a different tone and accent, each giving their earth name and earth address, each speaking to the correct sitter, each being recognised by the sitter, and each giving correct information relating to personal family affairs – Findlay had to question his own scepticism. His doubts were firmly cast aside when his own father spoke to him from the Spirit World. The voice referred to something that only Findlay knew. There was no way John was a fraud.

Findlay continued to research John's work. He transcribed thirty-nine different séances and documented two hundred and eighty-two separate communications. He classed one hundred and eighty of them as A1 (information that was impossible for the medium or any other person present to have known about), and one hundred were classed as A2 (information that could have been found in a newspaper or reference book).

Support from James Hewat McKenzie

James Hewat McKenzie was a British parapsychologist, and co-founder of the British College of Psychic Science, in London. He was also very interested in John's work. Desperate to make use of John's mediumistic skills, McKenzie found employment for him at a London garage. This arrangement continued for a number of years, and John was able to assist the college by becoming easily accessible to the various experimenters. John died in 1951.

CHAPTER TWENTY

Edgar Cayce

(1877-1945)

Edgar Cayce was an American healer, clairvoyant and trance medium. He was known as 'The Sleeping Prophet'.

Early Life

Cayce was born in Kentucky, USA. He was a very spiritual child and would often play with spirit children. He was an avid reader of the Bible – something he began to do at the age of ten. He had a hut in the woods, where he would sit and read. One day in 1889 he saw a woman with wings. He became afraid. When the woman asked him what he desired most in the world, Cayce told her he wanted to help others, especially sick children.

Following this episode, other strange things began to happen. Cayce would sleep and find on awakening that he had just absorbed the full contents of his school books. On one occasion, Cayce was struck on the base of the spine by a ball during a game of sport. He began to behave very strangely, and was put to bed. Whilst asleep, he was able to diagnose a cure for his injury: a cure that worked.

Disciple of Christ

Cayce finished school at ninth-grade and spent much of his younger years looking for work and money. He became involved in the Christian Church: Disciples of Christ, now called: The Christian Church, which is a mainline Protestant Christian denomination in the United

States and Canada. Cayce continued to read the Bible once a year, and even at this time was able to see auras around people and hear voices of departed relatives. But all this was overshadowed by a belief that his psychic abilities might *not* be coming from the highest source.

Illnesses and work

In 1900 Cayce contracted severe laryngitis, and lost the ability to speak. At first, he was unable to work, but finally turned to photography, which was not dependent on the power of his vocal cords. Cayce went on to seek the services of various hypnotists to see if his voice would return.

All attempts failed, until it was suggested by one of the hypnotists (Al Layne) that he link with the Spirit World, during hypnosis. Perhaps he would be told the problem, and given a cure. Cayce did this, and, whilst in trance, described the ailment: his loss of voice was due to psychological paralysis, and could be corrected by increasing the blood flow to the voice box. When Layne suggested that the procedure be carried out there and then, Cayce's face is said to have become flushed with blood, and both his chest and throat turned bright red.

The treatment worked, and with the exception of one or two relapses, Cayce's voice returned. As a result of this, Cayce, with the assistance of Layne, began to offer free trance healing to the public. This could be done in person, or by post (absent healing). He was able to diagnose physical and mental conditions, and then provide the cure.

Cayce continued to work like this all his life. Voluntary donations afforded him a living. In later years Layne was replaced by Cayce's wife, Gertrude. His secretary (Gladys Davis) was always there to record his trance readings in shorthand.

In 1923 Cayce was persuaded by Arthur Lammers (a wealthy printer, and student of metaphysics) to give trance readings on philosophical subjects. Metaphysics is the branch of philosophy that examines the fundamental nature of reality, including the relationship between mind and matter.

The Cayce Hospital

Cayce's medical remedies began to come under the scrutiny of the American Medical Association, so, he decided to legitimise his operations with the aid of licensed medical professionals. In 1929 the Cayce Hospital was established in Virginia Beach, but the depression years forced it to close its doors.

Spiritual Awareness

Cayce turned his attention to spiritual teachings. Eleven years of discourse with the Spirit World ensued, during which time, he discussed many subjects, including synchronicity: a subject that had first been introduced by the Swiss analytical psychiatrist, Carl Jung (1875 - 1961). Jung's work was influential in the fields of psychiatry, anthropology, archaeology, literature, philosophy, and religious studies. According to Jung, synchronicity is the same as meaningful coincidence, where events that are significantly related can take place simultaneously, but each event has happened for different reasons: cause differs, but effect is related.

Cayce also discussed intuition, which is the ability to know and to understand something without conscious reasoning. Often called the 'inner voice', it gives us the ability to tap into the guidance and knowing of our soul and subconscious. Karma was another topic, namely, the spiritual principle of cause and effect, where intent and actions of an individual (cause) influence the future of that individual (effect). The Akashic Records were also of interest to Cayce. These are a compendium of all human events, thoughts, words, emotions, and intents ever to have occurred in the past, present, or future. They are encoded in the ethereal plane, a non-physical place which is part of the cosmic whole: and we can access our own records through meditation. Cayce established many study groups, but always made it quite clear that their purpose was not to make you a medium, but to allow you to become a more spiritually aware and loving person.

CHAPTER TWENTY-ONE

Gladys Osborne Leonard

(1882-1968)

Gladys Osborne Leonard was one of the most investigated English mediums of the twentieth century.

Background

Gladys was born in Lytham St Annes. Her father was a wealthy yachting entrepreneur, so money, during her younger years, was no problem. She exhibited skills in mediumship from an early age, and later wrote that as a child she had visions of beautiful places: valleys, hills, trees and banks covered with flowers. She would also see happy people dressed in flowing garments. Unfortunately, when Gladys mentioned her visions to her family, she was forbidden to discuss the subject.

Financial Losses

As Gladys approached adolescence, her father underwent great financial losses. She was forced to review her life, and fend for herself. Since she had a beautiful singing voice, she began to work with opera and theatrical companies. She would sing and dance, tackling leading roles and comedy. It was during this time that she was told at a local Spiritualist church that her guides were preparing her for 'great spiritual work'.

Gladys' Mother dies

On 18 December 1906 Gladys awoke during the early hours with a strange feeling. When she looked up, she saw a large, circular patch of light, hovering five feet above her body. In the light was an image of her mother's face. The following day, she learned her mother had died.

Gladys investigates the Philosophy of Spiritualism

Shortly after her mother's death, Gladys married Frederick Leonard, a fellow thespian. The pair decided to live in the London area so that Gladys could do her research into psychic phenomena. Theatrical engagements were poorly paid, but Gladys accepted that this would be part of the course. In order to continue her research, she set up a group sitting with two sisters, Florence and Nellie. The three women would sit regularly, but it was not until their twenty-seventh sitting that anything happened. The table began to tilt up and down, and very soon they were able to use the tilting and the alphabet to spell out a series of evidential messages. It was during these séances that Gladys discovered that her guide was called 'Feda': a Hindu girl, who had married Gladys' great-great grandfather, William Hamilton. Feda had died, around 1800, after giving birth to a son. She was only thirteen years of age. As time progressed, Feda was able to put Gladys into trance: and so, began her life of dedicated service as a medium.

Sir Oliver Lodge and other psychical researchers

Gladys was one of the most investigated mediums of the twentieth century. For fifty years she gave remarkable evidence of personal survival to countless sitters. In 1915 she conducted a series of sittings with the renowned physicist, Sir Oliver Lodge and his wife, Lady Grace. Very soon, the information passed on by Gladys, convinced them that they were communicating with their son, Raymond, who had just been killed in the war. Sir Oliver put Gladys through stringent tests, but no matter what he did, the evidence kept flowing, until it became impossible to deny the obvious: Raymond lived on.

Sir Oliver wasn't the only psychical researcher who tested Gladys' work. Other researchers included, Reverend C. Drayton Thomas, James Hewat McKenzie and Whately Carrington. Still evidence was found, irrespective of the method used.

Book Test

Feda would direct the sitter to a certain book in a certain place in their home, where, on a given page, the sitter would find a special message.

Proxy Sittings

The person sitting with Gladys would be acting as a proxy on behalf of the actual sitter, who would be elsewhere. The sitter was known neither to the medium, nor to the person acting as a proxy – and still the sitter would be provided with the correct evidence.

Trance Mediumship

The way in which Gladys and Feda worked together was very interesting. Gladys was primarily a mental medium, but so too was Feda, who had to mentally reach out to the various spirit communicators in the Spirit World, and invite them to draw closer to the circle of energy-consciousness established around Gladys at the time of the sitting. Feda would then entrance Gladys and there would ensue a trance discourse. Gladys continued to work over the years with Feda. During this time, she set an example of honesty, integrity and professionalism.

CHAPTER TWENTY-TWO

Rebecca Beard

(1885-1952)

Rebecca Beard was an American medical practitioner who recognised the impact thought has on the physical body.

Early Research

For the first twenty years of her career, Rebecca led a fairly conventional life: that was until she began to notice the effect of thought and emotion on the health of the human body. She investigated her theory further, and soon determined that thought and emotion are largely responsible for many illnesses. She showed that by understanding thoughts and redirecting emotions, lives can be remoulded and bodies healed.

Spiritual Therapy

Rebecca turned to spiritual therapy, and prescribed fewer drugs. She recognised that medicines have their place, but said that when we learn that there is only one power behind all the agencies of healing, and choose to go directly to that power, we lose our dependence on drugs and the need for them. She said that dwelling on the negative will never make anything positive. We have to change the way we think and look for positive ways to achieve good aims.

Spreading the Word

Rebecca touched many lives. She said it was the birthright of every person to experience a sense of wholeness. In the summer months, she would stay in Merrybrook in Wells, Vermont, and continue her healing ministry. She engaged in group therapy and psychosomatic medicine (branch of medicine concerned with the interrelationships between mental and emotional reactions), and placed a strong emphasis on the power of prayer. During the winter months, she and her husband would travel from coast to coast, lecturing, counselling and engaging in the ministry of healing. Her philosophy still plays an influential part in the power of self-healing.

CHAPTER TWENTY-THREE

Frank Leah

(1886-1972)

Frank Leah is probably one of the best spirit artists the world has ever seen.

Early Life

Frank was a trained portrait and landscape artist and caricaturist. He sold his first cartoon to a newspaper when he was just twelve years old. When he was fifteen, he left home (Stockport) and went to Dublin, Ireland, where he started working for newspapers as an illustrator.

Art editor and animator

Frank became art editor for five journals, the *Weekly Freeman*, being one of them. He portrayed Irish theatrical personalities, and these have now been donated to the National Library of Ireland. In 1917, he was the animator on the first Irish animated film: *Ten Days' Leave*.

Psychic abilities

Frank decided to leave Ireland to develop his psychic skills and abilities to link with the Spirit World. Being clairvoyant (seeing Spirit), clairaudient (hearing Spirit) and clairsentient (sensing Spirit), he decided to work as a psychic/spirit artist in a studio in Kensington, London. He was able to see Spirit. His practice would be to draw what he could see and at the same time listen to what each spirit had to say about their human life and sense how they died.

He worked with Spirit for forty years and relayed many messages, bringing comfort to people after the loss of loved ones by providing evidence of survival of consciousness after physical death.

CHAPTER TWENTY-FOUR

Estelle Roberts

(1889-1970)

Estelle Roberts was a medium and healer.

Background

Estelle was born in Kensington, London. She was one of eight children and, as is the case of many mediums, began to sense Spirit from a very early age. Her family, however, would not accept this, and feared she was suffering from hallucinations. In adulthood, Estelle's mediumship included healing, psychometry, apports, clairvoyance, materialisation and direct voice.

Red Cloud

During the 1920s, Estelle attended the Spiritualist Church at Hampton Hill. She was told by one of the mediums that she was a medium, and had much work to do. She was further instructed to sit at home at a table, and wait for the Spirit World to make their presence known.

When she returned home, she began to do this, but nothing happened. She tried again for seven consecutive evenings. Still nothing happened, and she felt very foolish. However, as she turned away on the final evening, the table began to follow her within inches of her back. Realising that this was the proof she required, the proof that she was not hallucinating, she put her hand on the table and thanked the Spirit World.

It was then that she saw and heard her guide 'Red Cloud', for the first time. Red Cloud said that he was there to serve the physical world with her willing assistance.

Over the years, Estelle was always the first to point out that Red Cloud was good to her. She said that he treated her with gentleness and great consideration: and she was happy to serve. Red Cloud emphasised the importance of free will and personal responsibility.

Red Cloud speaks to Maurice Barbanell

Maurice Barbanell was a trance medium and writer. He channelled his spirit guide 'Silver Birch' for over sixty years, passing on wise philosophical information from the Spirit World. On one occasion, when Maurice attended one of Estelle's séances, Red Cloud came forward and told him that there was a girl (in Spirit) who wished to send a message to her mother. The girl began to speak through a spirit trumpet (a cone-shaped object used to amplify the sound of the spirit voice). She said that her name was Bessy Manning, and that she had died the previous Easter from tuberculosis. She added that her brother, Tommy, was with her, having been killed in a road accident.

Bessy further explained that her mother had been reading articles written by Maurice, and was praying that Red Cloud would bring her daughter, Bessy, to one of Estelle's séances. Bessy then said that her mother was to be told that she, Bessy, still had her two long plaits, that she was twenty-two and had blue eyes. She added that her mother was poor, and asked if they would bring her to one of their séances.

Of course, it has to be remembered that there is no 'Time' in the Spirit World as we understand it, and consciousness does not wear plaits, nor does it have blue eyes. But long plaits, blue eyes and an age of twenty-two would have had meaning to a mother still in the physical world: enough meaning to draw on memories and make sense of things.

More discussions took place, and it was agreed that the mother should be contacted and invited to the next séance. So, Mrs Manning was contacted. She was thrilled. Maurice made arrangements for her to attend the next séance, and Bessy came through again. When Bessy told her mother that Tommy was with her, Mrs Manning was delighted. Bessy also told her that she would often watch her from the Spirit World, and would see her pick up a photograph of her, talk to it, and kiss it.

Healing

Estelle's first patient was a young boy who arrived unexpectedly at Hampton Hill Spiritualist Church. He was suffering from a severe attack of asthma. Estelle silently appealed to Red Cloud to help her. She had no idea what would happen, but placing her hands on the child, put her faith in the Spirit World. The healing worked. Laboured breathing gradually became normal respiration, and that was the start of many years of healing work: all with the assistance of Red Cloud.

Psychometry

Estelle was very interested in psychometry. In her book, *Fifty Years a Medium*, she explained that psychometry is based on the fact that everything material pulses with vibrations, and that our auras also emanate vibrations, which are absorbed by inanimate objects nearby.

Experienced mediums handling such objects can translate the vibrations into a detailed description of the owner: character, idiosyncrasies and talents.

Police work

Estelle assisted the police on a few occasions, although she did find this work emotionally difficult, particularly murder cases, because of the horrific circumstances involved. Usually, she was reluctant to get involved in police enquiries because she was afraid her participation might be perceived as a stunt to advance herself at the cost of someone's tragedy. However, she did become involved in the investigation of one murder case in 1937: the abduction and murder of a child called Mona Tinsley. Estelle offered her services to the Chief Constable of Newark, but asked him to keep her involvement confidential. The Chief Constable agreed. Estelle asked him to send her some of Mona's clothing. Once Estelle received the clothing and handled it, she knew the child was dead, and in a clairvoyant image saw the location of the murder. All this information was given to the Chief Constable who asked her to come to Newark to see if she could be of further assistance.

Estelle took the train to Newark, and was picked up by car. On the drive to meet the Chief Constable, she passed a house and knew immediately that this was where the crime had been committed. Estelle was also able to point out areas where Mona had been, and these corresponded to where the police knew the child had been prior to the murder.

Estelle said Mona had been strangled, placed in a sack and carried away. Since the body had yet to be found, the Chief Constable pressed Estelle on where the body might be. Estelle asked the Chief Constable to walk with her. They passed a graveyard, where the police had been digging, and on to a field. Estelle told the Chief Constable that beyond the field was a river, and that was where Mona's body had been dumped.

The river referred to was the River Idle, which had already been dragged, but nothing found. Estelle, however, insisted that that was where the body would be found. Weeks later, the body was found in that river. Mona had been put in a sack, which had become jammed in a drain. The cause of death was strangulation.

The suspect for the crime was Fredrick Nodder. He was charged, convicted and eventually executed for the abduction and murder of Mona Tinsley. Although most of those involved in the investigation did their best to keep Estelle's part confidential, there was a leak somewhere, so Estelle is now included in the public records.

War

When the Second World War broke out in 1939, Red Cloud voiced his concerns, stating that man's physical fears were responsible for the war. As the war intensified, more and more war victims wanted to communicate with those they had left behind. Estelle began a wartime direct voice circle. The group of sitters included Air Chief Marshall, Lord Dowding, who was the head of Fighter Command during the Battle of Britain. Many young airmen, who had been shot down and died, came through, some of them known to Lord Dowding. Those who had not believed in life after death, were now very suitably surprised: and their reason for coming through was to prove to their loved ones that consciousness (spirit/soul) does indeed survive the death of the physical body.

CHAPTER TWENTY-FIVE

Eileen Jeanette Garrett

(1892-1970)

Eileen Garrett was a medium, who took an objective approach towards her own mediumship, and was closely investigated by the psychical researchers.

Background

Eileen Garrett was born in County Meath, Ireland. She was a natural sensitive (medium) from an early age, and as well as developing her mediumistic skills, went on to become a writer, editor, publisher, and one of the most important figures of the early parapsychological scene.

Eileen discovers auras

In her memoir: *Adventures in the Supernormal,* Eileen talks about auras and her attunement to nature. She describes how, as a child, she would see a nimbus of light (aura), shaped like an egg, round physical bodies. At the time, she called this light a 'surround'. Eileen would study the light, noting it consisted of transparent changing colours. Sometimes it would become dense and heavy in character, and would, in fact, change in accordance with the variations in people's moods. In other words, the aura revealed personality and feelings at a particular moment. Eileen found this very interesting. The blended lights of the nimbus-like covering showed how true claims of peace and amity in a relationship really were.

The more she studied the concept, the more she became fascinated by the impacts and reactions of thought. She could read the feelings of people when they met one another. But these 'surrounds' were not restricted to humans. She could see them encircle animals, plants and all organisms, and realised she could read the vitality of animals, shrubs, trees and much more. Over time, she became sure that animals sensed the emanations of each other: how otherwise did a rodent sense the presence of a hawk before even seeing it?

Eileen sees Spirit

Eileen started seeing spirit children when she herself was still a child. Visually, they were gauze-like, and light emanated from their substance. To touch them, they were soft and warm. Unfortunately, as happened with most child mediums, no one believed her. She soon discovered that the spirit children were an extension of nature. She had already learned to commune with trees, flowers and animals. Now she was communicating with spirit children by connecting with their energies.

Mediumship

Eileen's powers of telepathy (mind-to-mind communication) and clairvoyance were remarkable. She attracted world attention when she received a communication from the dead captain of Airship R101 after it crashed in 1931 – before the news was reported. R101 was part of a British government initiative to develop airships for passenger transport from Britain to India, Australia and Canada.

Investigating the science behind it all

Between 1924 and 1928, Eileen's psychic ability was further developed by James Hewat McKenzie, who was a Spiritualist and researcher at the British College of Psychic Science in London. Eileen took a very objective approach towards her abilities and enlisted the help of qualified researchers and scientists in investigating paranormal phenomena. In 1931, she was invited to the United States by the American Society for Psychical Research. During her visit, she went to Duke University, and worked under the guidance of William McDougall, who was a British psychologist, and J. B. Rhine, an American botanist who turned parapsychology into a branch of psychology.

Eileen and her researchers examined many areas within the wide spectrum of paranormal activity. Researchers included Alexis Carrel (a prominent French scientist, surgeon, humanitarian, and author), Nandor Fodor (a parapsychologist) and Hereward Carrington (an investigator of psychic phenomena). Topics investigated included telepathy and trance.

Further ventures

In 1941, Eileen started the publishing house Creative Age Press in New York. This was followed by Helix Press – another publishing house. She launched *Tomorrow Magazine*, which proved to be one of the most intelligent journals on paranormal topics of the time. In 1951 she set up the Parapsychology Foundation in New York. This was to encourage organised scientific research through grants and international conferences. It published the *International Journal of Parapsychology*, which ran from 1959 to 1968. Owing to popular demand, it resumed publication in 2000, but financial constraints and other events forced it to close after Volume 12.

CHAPTER TWENTY-SIX

Grace Cooke

(1892-1979)

Grace Cooke was a British medium.

Spiritualism and the White Eagle Lodge

Grace began her career as a medium in 1913. Between 1929 and 1931, the British Prime Minister, Ramsay MacDonald vouched for the accuracy of her readings. As time went on, however, Grace began to feel that the spiritual and philosophical aspects of Spiritualism were far more important than the evidence of survival after physical death. In 1936 she founded the White Eagle Lodge, under the inspiration of her Native American Indian spirit guide: White Eagle.

Teachings of White Eagle: Reincarnation

The Glasgow Association of Spiritualists is affiliated to the SNU (Spiritualists' National Union). One of the main differences between White Eagle's teachings and SNU Spiritualism, is the concept of reincarnation. The SNU feels there is insufficient evidence to prove this to be a conclusive reality. White Eagle, however, talks about man's different incarnations, which help to mould his personality. He also said that Jesus Christ was the son of God. Herein lies another difference. SNU Spiritualists accept that Jesus was *a* child of God, as we all are – but not *the* child.

CHAPTER TWENTY-SEVEN

Harry James Edwards

(1893-1976)

Harry Edwards was a well-known and respected healer.

Background

Harry was born in London: one of nine children. His father was a printer, his mother a dressmaker. He became a spiritual healer, teacher and author, with a career spanning nearly forty years.

Politics and the Army

Harry left school in 1907, and began a seven-year printing apprenticeship. But he became dissatisfied with the thought of a prospective career in printing, so turned his attention to politics and joined the Liberal Party. When World War I broke out in 1914, he enlisted in the Royal Sussex Regiment.

By late 1915, Harry was in Bombay on his way to Tikrit (Iraq), where he became part of the team building the railway track between Tikrit and Baghdad. During his time in the army, he reached the rank of Captain. In 1921 Harry returned to the UK and married Phyllis. He started his own printing business, but his attempts to launch himself back into a political career proved unsuccessful.

The Harry Edwards Healing Sanctuary

In 1935 Harry attended a meeting at a Spiritualist church. He was told by the medium present that he had healing powers. Harry followed the advice of the medium, and developed his skills in spiritual healing. His services were in great demand and his reputation spread.

In 1939, with the outbreak of World War II, Harry served in the Home Guard. He also continued to run his printing business: but that wasn't all. He'd already started to develop his own healing practice at home, which was doing very well. So well, that as his fame spread, his healing took over from his printing business.

Over time, the running of the business had to be passed on to his brother. In 1946 the number of patients visiting him continued to increase, so he moved his family and healing practice to a large house in Surrey. It had several acres of gardens and woodland, and it was here he founded: The Harry Edwards Healing Sanctuary.

Harry's healing

As Harry's fame spread, it was not uncommon for him to receive ten thousand letters a week, each one asking for help. Harry provided assistance using absent healing. Today, SNU healers work in accordance with the SNU Healing Code of Conduct, and are aware of the law as it relates to healing. A healer is not allowed to diagnose problems, prescribe medications, offer advice on treatment, or countermand a doctor's advice to a patient. All of these things are the responsibility of a qualified medical practitioner.

Harry's views

Harry's own views on spiritual healing were quite simple: the fact that healing works is far more important than trying to understand how it works. Notwithstanding, we should never close our minds to knowledge and understanding.

Harry and the animal kingdom

Harry not only believed in healing humans; he recognised the importance of healing animals. He said that animals are equally receptive to healing. They have souls: and their lives do not terminate with physical death.

CHAPTER TWENTY-EIGHT

Anthony Borgia

(1896-1989)

Anthony Borgia was a medium, who channelled the thoughts of a deceased priest: Monsignor Robert Hugh Benson.

Background

As a boy, Borgia had met Monsignor Benson, before the latter had died. A number of years later, following his death, Monsignor Benson went on to dictate scripts to Borgia. Many of these were converted into books. The Monsignor's main purpose was to correct the teachings contained in influential Christian books that had been written when he was living on earth. Indeed, some of these books had been written by the Monsignor, himself. He spoke about the Orthodox Christian Church, religious belief, faith, spirit communication, mediumship and existence in the Spirit World.

The Monsignor's views on psychic gifts

Monsignor Benson said that the Spirit World is full of spirit people, who, as humans, did not believe that we possess psychic abilities. Now they know that being psychic is part of our makeup, and we all possess an inherent power of mediumship – but this has to be developed. He added that the Orthodox Church is wrong to say that the dead cannot come back, or, wouldn't, if they could. The idea that those communicating through mediumship are 'devils' is total nonsense.

A final thought on the Orthodox Church and Belief

The Monsignor said that the Orthodox Church has assumed responsibility for the spiritual care of man on earth, but has failed in this task. It professes to know a great deal, but, in fact, knows very little in respect of man's wellbeing. It cannot provide answers to essential questions that are in the minds of most people.

CHAPTER TWENTY-NINE

Maurice Barbanell

(1902 - 1981)

Maurice Barbanell was a medium and writer.
His spirit guide was Silver Birch.

Early Years

Maurice's parents, Manel and Rifka, came from an area of Russian-speaking Poland, and moved to London around 1899. Manel set himself up as a barber in London's East End, where Maurice was born: one of six children. His first job was sweeping up hair and acting as lather boy for his father.

Introduction to Spiritualism

In his teens, Maurice became secretary of the Ghetto Social and Literary Club, a recreational club that had different interests. He later wrote that during his secretaryship, he was invited by friends to attend a séance. It turned out that this had been staged for fun. Unfortunately, the incident rendered him antagonistic towards Spiritualism.

However, things later changed. When a young Spiritualist, called Henry Sanders, asked Maurice to undertake a six-month period of personal investigation into Spiritualism, Maurice took up the challenge.

He was introduced to a home circle led by a Mrs Blaustein, who was a trance medium. Maurice was not impressed. However, when he attended the following week, matters turned a corner. Maurice believed he had fallen asleep. This was not the case. He had, in fact, gone into a deep trance and brought forward his guide, who was a North American Native Indian: Silver Birch.

Silver Birch

Silver Birch had passed to the Spirit World over three thousand years before. A highly evolved soul, he channelled spirit teachings from the Spirit World, using Maurice as his medium, by means of direct voice. It is believed that the information passed on by Silver Birch, actually came from a higher source; but because this higher consciousness functioned on a much higher vibration, then it would have to use the energy of Silver Birch to connect and pass on the information.

Teachings of Silver Birch

Silver Birch's philosophy is still an integral part of Spiritualism, today. He says that conventional (orthodox) theology cannot satisfy our minds and souls. He explains that we exist because we are spiritual beings expressing ourselves through a physical body. The spirit body is the supreme part, and each individual spirit is part of the spirit that created the whole universe. He likens the physical body to a house, and the spirit body, to a tenant. He emphasises the importance of looking after the 'house', meaning the physical body.

He also talks about the importance of differentiating between thought coming from the Spirit World, and our imagination. We all fit into a plan, but our path is governed by free will. We will have to face problems as a human being, but if we strive to do our best, we will receive spiritual guidance. This will help us to raise our spiritual awareness, which will not only help ourselves, but others. Silver Birch further explains that if we look at history, we will see that spiritual progress has proved difficult for mankind. War and conflict highlight this. Hostility, jealousy, greed and prejudice are all causes. Only kindness and compassion will help to overcome these.

Writing

In 1932, Maurice founded the newspaper, *Psychic News*, with the financial assistance of the psychical researcher and writer, Arthur Findlay. He left it for a period, then returned in 1962, as Editor, when it found itself in financial difficulties. He remained there until his passing in 1981. Maurice also took over the magazine: *Two Worlds* (founded by Emma Hardinge Britten in 1887).

Maurice wrote many books on Spiritualism, as did his wife, Sylvia. Maurice and Sylvia were both supported by influential colleagues, such as, Air Chief Marshall, Lord Dowding (distinguished RAF officer and psychical researcher), Sir Oliver Lodge (renowned physicist, inventor, writer and psychical researcher) and Sir Arthur Conan Doyle (physician, writer and psychical researcher).

CHAPTER THIRTY

Leslie Flint

(1911-1994)

Leslie Flint was a direct voice medium, and was probably one of the most tested in our time.

Background

Leslie had a very interesting background. He was little more than a toddler when the First World War broke out. His father was sent to fight and Leslie was left with his mother: but that was not an easy road. Mrs Flint liked to socialise. To begin with, she would leave Leslie alone, whilst she went out to consort with the local soldiers. When this was reported, she changed tactics. For a small fee, she would leave Leslie at the local cinema where the manager's wife would keep an eye on him. Unbeknown to Leslie at the time, the cinema would have a great bearing on his future life. Unfortunately, Mrs Flint was restless and decided to elope with a young soldier. Leslie was handed over to his grandmother, who lived in St Albans: a state-of-affairs that would have its ups and downs.

First psychic experience

One day, in the summer of 1918, Leslie's Aunt Nell came crying into his grandmother's kitchen. Her husband (Leslie's Uncle Alf) had just been killed in France. Leslie noticed that when his Aunt Nell came in, she was accompanied by a soldier, who was carrying Alf's belongings. But there was also another soldier, whom everyone was ignoring, even when he pulled at Nell's sleeves. Eventually, he simply disappeared. When Leslie was later shown a photograph of his Uncle Alf (whom he had never seen), he realised this was the man who had been pulling at Nell's sleeves. When he told his grandmother, she severely reprimanded him for 'telling lies'.

Second psychic experience

On returning home from school one day, Leslie could hear a conversation going on in the kitchen. When he went in, he found his grandmother. She was sitting sewing, and saying nothing. Next to her, however, was a lady, who had a mole on her chin. The moment Leslie looked at her, she disappeared. Leslie began to question his grandmother. The mole identified the woman as a certain Mrs Pugh: who was dead. Once again, Leslie received a severe reprimand, and was told to stop making up stories.

Rudolph Valentino

Leslie's first experience of a Spiritualist church was at the Friends' Meeting Place. Through time, a spirit purporting to be Rudolph Valentino, star of the Silver Screen, who had died in 1926, came forward and told Leslie that he would become a medium. Leslie was sceptical, but became less so when he received a letter from an unknown lady in Munich (Germany). The lady told him that Rudolph Valentino had given her Leslie's name and address, and had told her to write to him, reinforcing the fact that he was to develop his mediumship. Following this, Leslie was invited by a medium, Mrs Cook, to sit in a home circle, where he was able to witness physical mediumship: table movement and rapping. But that wasn't all. Rudolph Valentino returned and repeated his message.

Over time, other spirits also came through, and said that they wanted to experiment with the power in the room. They indicated that they hoped later on to use Leslie to speak in direct voice. But Leslie wasn't so sure. He was about to politely decline, when he received another letter from the lady in Munich. Valentino had come through again. He wanted to help Leslie develop his mediumship: a 'thank-you' for the affection he, himself, had experienced as a human being during his time in the physical world.

Independent direct voice

Leslie became an independent direct voice medium. This meant that the Spirit World did not work with his larynx (vocal cords), but used him as a vessel to produce their own voices, which came from an ectoplasmic larynx (invisible to the human eye, in most cases) and could be heard slightly above Leslie's head, and a bit to the side. The interesting thing was that Leslie did not have to go into trance. These voices were termed 'objective', because they could be heard by the sitters, many of whom, actually recorded the conversations. Voice tones ranged from a whisper to loud and recognisable: and very often the voices would speak to him on matters of philosophy and ethics.

The Zerdin Circle

Leslie was introduced to Noah Zerdin (founder of the Link Association of Home Circles), who invited him to join the Zerdin Home Circle. Leslie accepted, and his direct voice mediumship developed even further.

Over time, Leslie brought forward well-known scientists, such as, Thomas Edison, Sir Arthur Conan Doyle and Sir Oliver Lodge. These deceased individuals were personal friends of two of the sitters: a Dr Young and his wife.

Science and the afterlife

Dr Young was a scientist, and very interested in psychical research. He carried out many experiments to prove the authenticity of the voices produced during Leslie's direct voice sessions. Dr Young had been a close friend of Edison's, and knew about all the tricks fraudulent mediums would resort to. He'd travelled all over America and unmasked quite a few. His next task was to test Leslie. To do this, he tied him securely to a chair with a rope, and made him put a measured amount of coloured water into his mouth. The lights went out, and Leslie's control, Mickey, a cockney boy, came through loud and clear.

Twenty minutes later, the lights went back on. Leslie spat the water back into the jar: it was only slightly under the initial measurement.

Materialisation: physical phenomena

Materialised forms were beginning to appear during Leslie's mediumship. Dr Young suggested the use of a dim red bulb, so the sitters could see Leslie and the materialisations at the same time. This process proved successful. The materialised forms were solid and quite distinct from Leslie's own body, and could be felt and seen by the sitters.

The apparitions would move around the circle and communicate with some of the sitters. Leslie, who was not in trance, was conscious of what was going on, but his own body felt icy cold.

There was also a strange unpleasant smell. The Spirit World informed the circle that they were experimenting with Leslie's physical energy, but this form of phenomena was detracting from their ability to use his direct voice skills. The decision was finally made to concentrate on Leslie's ability to produce direct voice in order to bring comfort to the bereaved.

The Confraternity

This was a group of Christian clergymen, who believed in the reality of communication between the physical world and the Spirit World. The Reverend Charles Drayton Thomas was one of them. He would ask Leslie to sit for them. It was their aim to bring Spiritualism within the framework of the Christian Church. Unfortunately, they were faced with considerable hostility.

Hitler, the War and Edith Cavell

When the Second World War broke out in 1939, the Spirit World told Leslie that communications were being affected by the mass of negative energy surrounding the physical world. Nonetheless, Leslie struggled on with his direct voice mediumship. There were good days and bad days, but on one occasion, as he struggled with the heat inside his dark cabinet, the British nurse, Edith Cavell, came forward from the Spirit World. Edith had saved the lives of British and German soldiers in German-occupied Belgium, during the First World War. She had shown no discrimination, and had also helped around two hundred Allied soldiers escape back to Britain. The Germans had arrested her for this, and executed her. Now she had a very important message:

'However patriotic you might feel you must learn to love your enemy.'

As the Nazis continued to occupy Europe, Leslie became a conscientious objector, and when he was called up, he had to appear before a tribunal to state his case, and explain why he refused to take someone's life. It was finally agreed that he would be called into a non- combatant corps.

Society for Psychical Research

After the war, suggestions started to come from the Society for Psychical Research (SPR) that the voices were being produced by Leslie's own mouth, and that he was receiving his information clairaudiently. They wanted to carry out tests. The cabinet was checked for concealed microphones. There were none. Elastoplast was put over Leslie's tightly closed lips. A scarf was tied over this. His hands were then tied tightly to the arms of the chair, and another cord prevented him from lowering his head. Despite all this, his control, Mickey was soon speaking in a clear, coherent manner, bringing forth communicators, also speaking with clarity. At the end of the experiment, the bondage material was as tight as it had been.

The SPR tested for everything. Some believed he spoke from his stomach, others claimed the voices were not real voices, but through a combination of hypnotic powers on the part of Leslie, and a subconscious longing on the part of the sitters, auditory hallucinations were being induced. Someone even suggested that Leslie was some kind of super-ventriloquist-cum-mimic. And so, the tests continued. Leslie's mouth was sealed. A microphone was attached to his throat to amplify any sounds he might make. An infrared telescope allowed the researchers to watch him in the cabinet. His hands were held by a sitter on either side of him. But still the voices were heard, and the telescope was even able to pick up the ectoplasmic larynx, two feet away from him.

Professor Charles Richet

During one of Leslie's sittings, a French voice came through. The spirit identified itself as Professor Charles Richet, who had been an eminent French physiologist, and a president of the Society for Psychical Research in London in 1905. Richet explained how the Spirit World was able to use Leslie's mediumship. Leslie and other physical mediums had a great deal more ectoplasm than the ordinary person. During a séance, the ectoplasm would be drawn from Leslie, and the Spirit World was able to use it to create a spirit larynx. The communicating spirit would then concentrate its thoughts into this voice box, and this would create a vibration that would reach the sitters in the form of an objective sound. Each spirit would have to lower its vibration and remember the voice they had had when in the physical body. And not only that – it was essential that each spirit recaptured memories in order to pass them on to the sitters.

CHAPTER THIRTY-ONE

Albert Best

(1917-1996)

Albert Best was an Irish medium, who was well known for the very accurate evidence he gave during his demonstrations of mediumship.

Early Life

Albert was born in Belfast, Northern Ireland. His mother died when he was young, so he was brought up by his grandmother, who was a staunch Protestant, and her four daughters, whom he referred to as sisters.

During his childhood, Albert sensed, heard and saw Spirit, but it frightened him. His earliest experience was at the age of seven, when he saw a man standing at the top of his grandmother's stairs, carrying a lit lamp. Albert noticed that the man had tied string around his legs just below the knees (he later discovered that this was to stop rats and mice running up his legs when cutting the fields of cereal crops). When Albert told his grandmother about the man, she brushed him off, telling him that he'd eaten too much cheese. However, as he left the room, he heard his grandmother speak to the man, referring to him as her father. He also heard her 'shoo him away', telling him he was frightening 'the boy'. The realisation that this man was his deceased grandfather, whom he'd never met, meant that Albert was no longer afraid of the Spirit World.

Albert visits his first Spiritualist Church

Albert's grandmother died before he left school. Her four daughters (his aunts) had already moved out, so Albert went to live with one of them. It was at this time, he decided to visit a Spiritualist church, where he was told by the platform medium that he would wear a uniform and go to Africa. This message would have a great deal of significance later on in his life.

Albert leaves school

When he was fourteen years of age, Albert started work in a rope factory. It was also at this time that he would go for long walks in the countryside to be alone with the spirit voices. They brought him comfort and reassurance and would help guide him in his day-to-day life.

Albert gets married

When Albert met Rose, the girl of his dreams, he discovered that she was a Catholic. Since religious bigotry predominated in Northern Ireland, this clearly posed a problem. But the pair didn't care: they were in love. Within a few months of meeting, they went to St Anne's Cathedral in Belfast to see the priest, and married: no relatives present.

The Second World War

In 1939, with the outbreak of World War II, Albert decided to join the Inniskilling Fusiliers, whilst Rose stayed in Northern Ireland with her family in the Belfast area (New Lodge). In 1940, Albert found himself in Algiers, North Africa. So, the medium had been right when she had said he would wear a uniform and go to Africa. In 1943, during a battle with the Germans on the Goubellat Plain (Tunisia), he recalled something his other grandmother had once said, the only time they had ever met, when he had been aged fourteen years. She had told him that he would be a widower by the age of twenty-four, and that she would see him in Goubellat.

Albert was injured during the battle, but escaped capture. He did, however, end up as a prisoner of war at a later date – an experience he never discussed. Sadly, his other grandmother's prediction came true. Rose was still at home in Belfast with their three children whilst Albert was in Africa. When he was released from captivity, he was sent home, only to find that his family had been completely wiped out in a massive bombing.

Albert goes to Scotland

Albert was discharged from the Army in 1943, when he was 25 years of age. In 1944, he moved to Irvine (Ayrshire, Scotland). He became the local postman and formed a friendship with a Spiritualist family (George and Olive Williamson and their daughter). Through this family, he met other Spiritualists and joined a development circle, where he remained for two years. In 1951 Albert joined a development circle at Kilmarnock Church. He sat with this circle until the mid-fifties, never once discussing his private life. When he was introduced to Maurice Barbanell, he was able to develop even further.

Albert's Mediumship

Albert was well known for the very accurate evidence he gave during his demonstrations of mediumship. It was clear the Spirit World had decided to make good use of his experience as a postman, meaning he was regularly able to give names and addresses, along with other private details. Recipients of his messages were in awe as Albert constantly proved that consciousness survives the death of the physical body.

Spiritual Healing

Albert's skills were not restricted to demonstrations of clairvoyance and clairaudience, he was an excellent healer. He had three spirit helpers: 'Dr Wong', 'Hans' and 'Ally', and worked as a trance healing medium in his healing sanctuary.

Albert travels abroad

Albert's work took him to many different countries, including Africa and India. It is widely reported that whilst in Africa, Albert visited a witch doctor, and during a ritual, his wife, Rose, materialised, then dematerialised, providing evidence that she lived on.

Spiritualist of the Year

In 1994, Roy Stemman, chairman of the *Psychic Press*, made a presentation to Albert at the Lewisham Theatre in London, naming him 'Spiritualist of the Year'.

CHAPTER THIRTY-TWO

Gordon Higginson

(1918-1993)

Gordon Higginson was a mental and physical medium, specialising in direct voice and materialisation.

Early Life

Gordon was born in Longton, Stoke-on-Trent. His spiritual development began at a very early age. His mother, Fanny, was a medium, and Gordon began sitting in her circle when he was three years of age. He was not, however, allowed to give a message until he reached the age of ten years.

On his twelfth birthday, Gordon gave his first public demonstration of mediumship at Longton Spiritualist Church: and embarked on a very successful career.

Platform Mediumship

Gordon was renowned for the accuracy of his platform mediumship. His evidence often included full names, addresses and telephone numbers.

Physical Mediumship

Not only was Gordon a mental medium, he was also an excellent physical medium. His skills included direct voice and materialisation. Also, transfiguration, which is where the Spirit World can mould a spirit mask over the medium's face. The mask resembles the features of the communicating spirit, such as it appeared as a human being. Gordon would demonstrate these types of phenomena publicly to audiences of up to three hundred people.

Gordon's guides and helpers

During his childhood, Gordon's spirit friend, Cuckoo and his Irish guide, Paddy, provided great fun for him. Paddy also assisted him with clairvoyance, whilst in the trance state. His principal guide was Choo Chow, who provided spiritual words of wisdom. Another guide, Light, would pop in at Christmas.

Healing

Gordon was a great healer. Queues would regularly form outside Longton Spiritualist Church whenever he held healing sessions. With the assistance of his healing guide, Dr John, he was able to diagnose and provide healing for a wide range of ailments: for humans and animals.

Longton Spiritualist Church

In 1946, Gordon became president of Longton Spiritualist Church. He held this position until his passing in 1993.

Stansted Hall

In 1965 Gordon taught at the very first Summer School at the Arthur Findlay College, Stansted Hall. In 1979, he became Principal of the College, remaining in that position until 1993.

During that time, he gave many demonstrations of mediumship. He was also a fine and eloquent speaker. His addresses contained style and charisma. They also demonstrated his love and passion for Spirit. Many people came to hear his lectures at Stansted Hall, and very often he would give demonstrations of physical mediumship in the College Library.

Spiritualists' National Union

In 1970, he became president of the Spiritualists' National Union (SNU). At this time, the Union was in severe financial crisis, and had been given less than two years to survive. Stansted Hall (its registered office) was also in debt. Gordon's energy and determination saved the Union from bankruptcy, and cleared the debt owed by Stansted Hall (Arthur Findlay College). Gordon was also a minister of the SNU, and officiated many naming, wedding and funeral services. He is now an honorary president in Spirit of the SNU.

Glasgow Association of Spiritualists

In 1972 Gordon held a physical séance in front of over two hundred people at Somerset Place. During the séance, loved ones materialised and spoke in direct voice to friends and relatives in the congregation. It proved to be a sensation. Gordon was also an honorary president of the Glasgow Association of Spiritualists.

Psychical Researchers

CHAPTER THIRTY-THREE

Alfred Russel Wallace

(1823 - 1913)

Alfred Russel Wallace was a scientist, who researched Spiritualism and wrote extensively on the subject.

Background

Alfred was born in the Welsh village of Llanbadoc. He became a naturalist, geographer, anthropologist and biologist. Alfred was also a social activist. He criticised the unjust social and economic system in Britain, and was one of the first prominent scientists to raise concerns over the human impact on the environment.

Spiritualism

Alfred began investigating Spiritualism in 1865. He reviewed literature and attempted to test what he witnessed at séances. He remained convinced that at least some séances were genuine, albeit he understood that some were influenced by trickery. He felt that Spiritualism was a matter of science and philosophy rather than religious belief.

Conclusions

Alfred reached four conclusions:

- A human being's individual existence extends beyond biological death.

- Conscious existence during this period is determined by the level of intellectual and moral development during one's life.

- Intellectual and moral development is a function of free will.

- There is a continuity of cause and effect in nature which cannot be avoided.

Charles Darwin

Alfred is probably best known for independently conceiving his *Theory of Evolution*, but he always took a back seat. When Charles Darwin saw how much Alfred's theory of natural selection matched his own, he published a joint paper with him. The following year, Darwin published his own work: *Origin of Species*. Alfred and Charles Darwin wrote cordially to one another for many years, but did not agree on everything. Darwin could not accept the philosophy behind Spiritualism. He did not believe that the human spirit persists after death, nor would he accept Alfred's belief that natural selection cannot explain the human intellect.

Alfred's advocacy of Spiritualism damaged his scientific reputation and affected public perception of his work, but that did not stop him standing by his convictions. He was a tireless thinker and wrote widely on Spiritualism and other topics, including land ownership, workers' rights, law, economics and museums. He was never able to secure a permanent position and ended his days marking government examinations, and writing papers for small sums. He also helped Darwin edit his work: for a fee.

Medals

Despite his back seat, Alfred was awarded probably every important medal possible for a biologist in Britain at that time. These medals included the Darwin–Wallace medal, presented to him in 1908.

CHAPTER THIRTY-FOUR

Sir William Crookes

(1832-1919)

Sir William Crookes was an eminent British professor of science and psychical researcher.

Background

Sir William discovered Thallium (a chemical element with the symbol Tl and atomic number 81), and invented the radiometer, which was a device for measuring the radiant flux of electromagnetic radiation. Also the spinthariscope: a device for observing individual nuclear disintegrations; and the Crookes Tube: an early experimental electrical discharge tube, with partial vacuum, in which cathode rays (streams of electrons), were discovered.

Awards

1863:	Elected a Fellow of the Royal Society.
1875:	Royal Society's Royal Gold Medal for chemical and physical research.
1888:	The Davy Medal.
1897:	Knighted by Queen Victoria.
1904:	The Sir Joseph Copley Medal.

Psychical Research: Florence Cook

Sir William set out to disprove the existence of psychic and physical phenomena, believing it was a trick. He felt it was the duty of scientists to make such investigations, and discover the truth. Florence Cook (see Chapter 16) was a British physical medium, best known for her skills in materialisation, particularly with regard to a spirit called Katie King, and it was reserved for Sir William to prove her integrity, or, otherwise. He finally published a report in 1874 confirming her authenticity. The report was met with ridicule and protest. Allegations were made that Florence and Katie King were one and the same, but Sir William provided evidence proving that this could not be the case.

Electrical tests

Sir William went on to use an electrical test devised by the Royal Society. Florence was placed in an electric circuit, connected with a resistance coil and a galvanometer. Nothing suspicious occurred, yet Katie appeared, waved her arms about, shook hands with her friends and wrote in their presence. When the séance was over, the wires were found attached to Florence exactly as they had been at the start; and on examination, the galvanometer showed no signs of violent fluctuations.

CHAPTER THIRTY-FIVE

Henry Sidgwick

(1838-1900)

Henry Sidgwick was an English philosopher and economist.

Background

Sidgwick's career was varied. He became Knightbridge Professor of Moral Philosophy at the University of Cambridge. He was also a supporter of the higher education of women, and helped to open a house of residence for female students, which became Newnham College, Cambridge.

Parapsychology

Henry Sidgwick had a lifelong interest in the paranormal. His interest, combined with his personal struggles with religious belief, prompted him to form a group of like-minded individuals, which became known as the 'Sidgwick Group'. In 1882, the Sidgwick Group developed into the Society for Psychical Research, and Sidgwick was its first president.

Eleanor Sidgwick

In 1876 Sidgwick married Eleanor Mildred Balfour, who was a member of the 'Ladies Dining Society' (private women's dining and discussion club) at Cambridge University. Eleanor was the sister of Arthur Balfour: Prime Minister of Great Britain from 1902 -1905. Balfour, interestingly, also became a member of the Society for Psychical Research, and was its president from 1892 to 1894. Eleanor was another leading figure in the Society. She was elected its president in 1908, and named president of honour in 1932. Most of Eleanor's writing related to psychical research, and can be found in the book: *Proceedings of the Society for Psychical Research.*

CHAPTER THIRTY-SIX

Frederic William Henry Myers

(1843 - 1901)

Frederic Myers was a classical scholar, poet and philosopher.

Background

Myers was educated at Cheltenham College and Trinity College, Cambridge. He later became a lecturer at Trinity College, and whilst there, met Professor Henry Sidgwick, who became one of his most valued friends. Myers joined Sidgwick as an active promoter of women's higher education.

Psychical Research

Myers was very interested in telepathy, Spiritualism and Mesmerism. He became one of the founding members of the Society for Psychical Research (SPR) in 1882, becoming its president in 1900. Myers was a Spiritualist, but kept an open mind in relation to the physical mediums he investigated. He believed that although many of them cheated, others could produce genuine physical phenomena.

Myers was certain his research provided the evidence for the existence of the soul, and survival of personality after death. His works cited cases of automatic writing, hypnotism, mediumship, poltergeist activity, psychokinesis and telepathy.

In his book, *Human Personality and Its Survival of Bodily Death*, he talks about the existence of a metetherial world (Spirit World), which he says is a world of images, lying beyond the physical world. He stresses that apparitions are not hallucinations, but have a real existence in the metetherial world, and that these apparitions occupy regions of physical space.

CHAPTER THIRTY-SEVEN

Sir William Fletcher Barrett

(1844-1925)

Sir William Fletcher Barrett was an English physicist and parapsychologist.

Background

Sir William was born in Kingston, Jamaica, where his father (William Garland Barrett: Congregationalist minister and member of the London Missionary Society), ran a station for saving African slaves. In 1848, his family returned to Hertfordshire, England. In 1855, they moved to Manchester, where Sir William was educated at Old Trafford Grammar School. He went on to study chemistry and physics at the Royal College of Chemistry. Between 1867 and 1869, he was science master at the London International College, which took in international students in an attempt to foster good relations between different countries, and prevent war. This was followed by positions at the Royal Institution and the Royal School of Naval Architecture. In 1873, he became Professor of Experimental Physics at the Royal College of Science for Ireland.

Study of Metals

Sir William undertook considerable research into metals and their properties. One of his discoveries was Stalloy, a silicon-iron alloy used in electrical engineering.

Cataracts

When he developed cataracts in his later years, he decided to study biology and conducted a series of experiments, designed to locate and analyse causative agents within the eyes. From these experiments, he produced a machine called the Entoptiscope, which has since developed into the blue field Entoptiscope.

Awards

Sir William was elected a Fellow of the Royal Society (London), a Fellow of the Royal Society of Edinburgh and the Royal Dublin Society, and he was knighted in 1912 for his contributions to science.

Psychical Research

During the 1860s, Sir William underwent various paranormal experiences involving Mesmerism and thought transfer. By the 1870s, he had completed extensive psychical research, including the investigation of poltergeist activity. In September 1876, he published a paper outlining the results of his experiments. By 1881, he had published preliminary accounts of additional experiments with thought transference in the journal, *Nature*. His articles caused controversy, but Sir William was not deterred.

Sir William was a Christian and Spiritualist, and recognised the value of founding a society of like-minded people. In January 1882 he held a conference in London. By February, the Society for Psychical Research (SPR) was formed. He also became active in the Dublin Section of the SPR, and in 1884 he founded the American Society for Psychical Research, becoming its president in 1904.

Dowsing

Sir William was especially interested in divining rods to detect energy vibrations. He concluded that in some cases, the dowser's unconscious mind could pick up information by clairvoyance.

Lady Barrett

In 1916, Sir William married Florence Willey, a British medical doctor. Although Lady Barrett shared Sir William's interest in psychical research, she was already a pioneer in her own right, and was one of the leading gynaecologists and obstetricians of her time. She was a consultant surgeon at the Mothers' Hospital in Clapton, which was a hospital for unmarried mothers.

She was also a consultant at the Royal Free Hospital in London, which was, at the time, the only hospital in England where women could train in medical practice. In 1916, she led a fundraising campaign to extend the hospital, adding maternity, paediatric and infant welfare facilities. She then went on to help develop the London School of Medicine for Women, becoming dean, and subsequently, president. She also established voluntary centres in London to provide food for undernourished children and pregnant women, and was an avid supporter of Women's Suffrage and equal employment rights for women.

During the 1920s, when she worked at the Mothers' Hospital, Lady Barrett recorded accounts of women having 'deathbed visions' before they died, following childbirth complications. Their accounts convinced her that they were seeing the spirits of deceased relatives, or, friends, who were appearing to reassure the dying women, and welcome them to the next world. Lady Barrett's observations led Sir William to do his own research in this area, which he compiled in the book: *Deathbed Visions*. After Sir William died in 1925, Lady Barrett used the services of a medium to conduct a series of conversations with him. She published a book in 1937 (*Personality Survives Death*) which records these conversations.

CHAPTER THIRTY-EIGHT

Edmund Gurney

(1847 - 1888)

Edmund Gurney was a classical scholar and psychical researcher.

Background

Gurney was born at Hersham, near Walton-on-Thames, England, educated at Trinity College, Cambridge and given a place in the Classical Tripos. He obtained a Fellowship in 1872. Gurney was a gifted musician, and in 1880 wrote an essay on the philosophy of music: *The Power of Sound*. He studied medicine, with no intention of practising, devoting himself to physics, chemistry and physiology. In 1880 he passed the second M.B. Cambridge (medical science), and in 1881 he studied Law.

Psychical Research

In 1875, three of Gurney's sisters had died when their barge overturned on the Nile River, during a tour of Egypt. Their passing profoundly affected him, and his psychical research was partially fuelled by a desire to find some meaning to their deaths. In 1882, the Society for Psychical Research was founded, and Gurney went on to devote his time to research along with other notable researchers of the time: Frederic Myers, Sir William Barrett, Henry Sidgwick and Sir Oliver Lodge.

CHAPTER THIRTY-NINE

Charles Richet

(1850-1935)

Charles Richet was a French physiologist.

Background

Richet studied in Paris and earned a Medical Degree in 1877. He became Professor of Physiology in 1887. He published many works, and was Editor of the journals: *Revue Scientifique* (Science Review) and *Journal de Physiologie et de Pathologie Generale* (Journal of Physiology and General Pathology). He also published papers on physiology, physiological chemistry, and experimental pathology.

In 1913 he won the Nobel Prize for his research into anaphylaxis (severe, life-threatening allergic reactions).

Psychical Research

Charles Richet was extremely interested in Spiritualism, and investigated a wide spectrum of phenomena, including hypnosis, telepathy, psychokinesis and ectoplasm.

Ectoplasm

Richet created the word 'ectoplasm'. It comes from the Greek 'ektos' and 'plasma': exteriorised substance. Ectoplasm is dynamic energy. It is invisible and intangible in its primary state, but can assume a vaporous and solid state. It can emit a smell, which may be unpleasant, and can be drawn from the body of a medium. It is able to assume various semi-solid and solid states. These can be felt, and under certain circumstances, photographed. When vaporous, it can resemble fog, or, a slightly phosphorescent mist. When solid, it can appear in the form of a full human body, or, just the fingers, hands and face. It then disintegrates and disappears and is reabsorbed back into the medium's body. It has been seen in various aspects in red light and good white light, and has been photographed many times by investigators.

CHAPTER FORTY

Sir Oliver Lodge

(1851-1940)

Sir Oliver Lodge was a professor of physics and mathematics.

Background: Science

Sir Oliver was born in Staffordshire, England and educated at Adams' Grammar School in Newport, Shropshire. At the age of fourteen he began to work for his father's company (Oliver Lodge & Son), selling Purbeck blue clay to the potteries. He worked there until the age of twenty-two, when he decided to attend physics lessons in London and study at the local Wedgewood Institute.

In 1875, he obtained a Bachelor of Science degree from London University, and in 1877, a Doctor of Science. That same year, he married Mary Marshall, and they went on to have twelve children. (Four of his sons later went into business using Sir Oliver's inventions: sparking plugs for cars and aeroplanes, and an electrostatic device for cleaning factory and smelter smoke.)

In 1881 he became Professor of physics and mathematics at University College, Liverpool. In 1900 he moved back to the Midlands and took on the post of the first Principal of the new Birmingham University. In 1898 he was awarded the Rumford Medal of the Royal Society, and in 1902, was knighted by King Edward VII. Sir Oliver retired from Birmingham University in 1919, and was made Freeman of his native city (Stoke-on-Trent) in 1928.

Background: Psychical Research

Sir Oliver was a member of the Ghost Club and from 1901 to 1903 served as president of the London-based Society for Psychical Research (SPR).

Electromagnetic waves

In 1879, Sir Oliver became interested in the generation and detection of electromagnetic waves. He conducted research, but was 'pipped at the post' by Heinrich Hertz, who was the first to demonstrate the transmission and receipt of controlled radio waves. Sir Oliver then decided to investigate lightning. To do this, he attached a long wire to a Leyden jar. When the room was darkened, he noticed a glow, at intervals, along the wire, like lightning, evidence that he was observing electromagnetic waves.

Telepathy

Many people in the Victorian era firmly believed in telepathy. Sir Oliver first began to study psychical phenomena during the late 1880s and deduced that mind reading might be a form of communication through the ether, rather like radio waves.

Spiritualism

Sir Oliver was a Christian Spiritualist, who believed that life after death had been proved by mediumship. When his son, Raymond was killed in 1915 during World War I, he visited several mediums, principally, Gladys Osborne Leonard (see Chapter 21), and wrote about the experience in a number of books. Sir Oliver also endorsed a theory of spiritual evolution: that religious teachings about God were compatible with scientific understanding of biological evolution.

CHAPTER FORTY-ONE

James H. Hyslop

(1854-1920)

James Hervey Hyslop was a professor of Ethics and Logic at Columbia University (USA).

Background

Professor Hyslop was also a psychologist, and was one of the first to connect psychology and psychic phenomena.

Psychical Research

Hyslop began to carry out psychical research during the 1880s. When ill health forced him to retire from his teaching post, his interest in the subject increased. He became actively involved in the work of the American Society for Psychical Research (ASPR). He was also a member of the London-based Society for Psychical Research (SPR).

In 1904, he went on to found the American Institute for Scientific Research to raise funds for psychical research. He established two branches, one that focused on abnormal psychology and one that centred on psychical research.

In 1905, the existing ASPR was dissolved, and in 1906, the psychical research branch of the American Institute became a new independent ASPR, replacing the original Institute.

Mental Mediumship

Hyslop started out as an agnostic – but his views soon changed. Much of his work was with the Boston medium, Leonora Piper (see Chapter 17). Her abilities impressed him. He believed that through her, he had received messages from his father, his wife and other members of his family. He reported this in: *Journal of the Society for Psychical Research* (London, 1901). He continued to make his views about the Spirit World very clear, particularly in his book: *Life After Death*.

CHAPTER FORTY-TWO

Sir Arthur Conan Doyle

(1859-1930)

Sir Arthur Conan Doyle was a British writer and physician.

Background

Sir Arthur was born in Picardy Place, Edinburgh, Scotland, and educated at the University of Edinburgh Medical School.

Sherlock Holmes

He began his writing career with fiction. He chronicled the adventures of his two main characters (Sherlock Holmes and Dr John Watson), and went on to write novels, short stories, plays, poems and works of non-fiction.

Laws of the Universe

Sir Arthur began to question the Laws of the Universe when he finished his medical training in 1882. He believed in an intelligent force, but wasn't convinced the human brain could ever understand more than that. He felt the concept of right and wrong needed no explanation, but when it came to the survival of consciousness, there seemed nothing to support such a thing. However, following the close successive deaths of his son and brother, Sir Arthur began to examine Spiritualism: and never looked back.

Society for Psychical Research

In 1891, Sir Arthur joined the London-based Society for Psychical Research, and was given access to many reports and accounts of psychic phenomena. He researched the subject, and was surprised to find that many well-known scientists were also studying it, and agreeing that not only were the spirit and physical body separate: the spirit could survive the physical body.

To begin with, Sir Arthur could find no scientific explanation of what was happening, until he read a book by a fellow psychical researcher, Frederic Myers. The book was called: *Human Personality and Its Survival of Bodily Death*. Sir Arthur found it provided excellent examples of mind-to-mind communication (telepathy). It also helped him to take a step forward in his research, and provided an answer to his previous doubts: if the mind could act independently of the physical body, then why should it not survive the physical body?

Sir Arthur was slowly realising that there had to be laws and forces existing which had never been examined by science. Not only that, evidence was highlighting that although scientists and religious experts were, in their own right, examining Spiritualism, to his knowledge, neither group had ever tried to connect the two disciplines: this was something he had to investigate.

Science v Religion

Many of the scientists, including Sir William Barrett, believed that psychical research and religion were two different things, but Sir Arthur begged to differ.

He believed that evidence produced from psychical research was teaching humankind how to behave, and since this would affect development in the Spirit World, then the two could not be separated. But there was one great difference: Spiritualism should not be treated as another religion (there were already enough out there) it was to be used as a basis to unify all religions.

The Spirit World

Sir Arthur's research led him to write the book: *The New Revelation*. In this book, he describes how, on death, individuals find themselves in a spirit body that stands, or, floats next to their deceased physical body. The spirit is conscious of the physical body, as well as the physical bodies of those people standing nearby. However, when the spirit tries to communicate with those on the physical plane, in the majority of cases, it cannot, for the vibrations of the Spirit World are much finer than those of the physical world.

The room then fills with long departed family and friends, who welcome the spirit of the newly deceased; they guide the spirit to its place in the Spirit World. The spirit is surprised to find how its much finer form can glide easily through hard physical objects. The truth then becomes evident: Spirit is not a glorified angel or damned creature, as described in the Bible, but simply the same person whose personality does not change.

Sir Arthur goes on to describe how the spirit must heal before it is ready to continue with the next stage of life. Heaven and Hell are not places, but states of mind, and the state of mind depends on the level of personal development during the physical life. If the spirit has led a 'bad' life, it will be placed on a lower sphere, with a lower vibration, where it must learn to develop in a positive fashion. It will be given the opportunity to progress through the spheres. It can generally be found that spirit communicators are not too many generations away from their human loved ones, and will stop communicating once all those dear to them have crossed over to the Spirit World.

Sir Arthur continues to explain that there are many levels of development in the Spirit World, and that there is more communication between these different levels than there is between the Spirit World and the physical world. The lower levels (lower vibration) in the Spirit World cannot ascend to communicate, but the higher levels (higher vibration) can descend. This does not mean physical displacement: instead, it involves the lowering of vibrational frequencies to permit blending. The physical world is a life of the physical body, and the Spirit World is a life of the mind. Spirits live in communities of like-minded energies. There is no sex or childbirth. Language is no longer a barrier, for thought becomes the means of communication, and the means for constructing new lives.

On death, it is usual for the newly deceased to think they are dreaming. This can have a debilitating effect on development, and take time to redress. For that reason, accurate knowledge of the Spirit World, before death, would better prepare humankind. The Spirit World might appear dream-like to the denser human being, but it is actually suitably constructed, and very much in harmony with the needs of a finer, lighter entity, allowing us to continue on our individual paths in search of our own positive goals.

Sir Arthur emphasises that Spiritualism is not a new thing, but a rediscovery of what has always been there. He adds that there is such a preponderance of evidence, that it is time for the physical world to ask itself why exactly it is being shown the evidence, and explore and discover the true meaning of life, both here and in the Spirit World. Furthermore, he wants us to understand that Spiritualism shows us that by treating others in a respectful and unselfish manner, we will progress. Life continues after physical death, so we can continue this progression. But we should remember: never impose it on others. We each have our own personal path, and it is up to us, as individuals, to examine our own principles, as we pursue our own quest for personal development.

CHAPTER FORTY-THREE

Gustav Geley

(1865-1924)

Gustav Geley was a French physician and psychical researcher.

Background

Geley was born in Montceau-les-Mines, France and studied Medicine at Annecy. As well as having a career in Medicine, he was a psychical researcher. In 1919, he gave up his practice as a physician, and became Director of the Institut Metaphysique International, which was the French equivalent of the Society for Psychical Research. He investigated many cases of physical mediumship and wrote papers on the subject. He was also a Spiritualist and a believer in reincarnation.

Ectoplasm

Like Charles Richet, Geley was interested in the composition of ectoplasm. In 1921, he concluded that ectoplasm is a physical extension of the medium, which may appear solid or vaporous, and can take on an organic form, producing forms which can have the anatomical and physiological characteristics of living organs.

CHAPTER FORTY-FOUR

Reverend Charles Drayton Thomas

(1867-1953)

Reverend Charles Drayton Thomas was a Methodist minister, Spiritualist and psychical researcher.

Background

Charles Drayton Thomas was born in Taunton, Somerset (England). In 1889, he entered Richmond Theological College, and from 1892 to 1907 served various Methodist circuits in England. When he gave this up, he took a position at the Leysian Mission (London). Here, most of his work was centred round the poverty-stricken areas, and he focussed most of his attention on the social and housing conditions in the East End of London.

Reverend Thomas was not like other ministers. He was a member of the Society for Psychical Research, and a convinced Spiritualist. He devoted a major portion of his life to systematic psychic study.

Psychical Research

As a minister, Reverend Thomas had for many years been interested in the subject of life after death. In 1917, he had his first sitting (anonymously) with the medium, Gladys Osborne Leonard (see Chapter 21). He went on to attend séances with her, carrying out many experiments. In 1922 he began publishing a long series of books and articles, in which he presented cumulative evidence (through the mediumship of Mrs Leonard) that he was in full communication with his father and sister, as well as with other departed friends. He always kept full and annotated records of his sittings. He also made gramophone recordings of some of the communications from his father and made everything available to other psychical investigators. Mrs Leonard and her sitters entered well into the spirit of scientific investigation.

Reverend Thomas was able to collate his evidence from multiple sources and tests. He investigated direct voice utterances (defending the direct voice medium, Leslie Flint, despite the fact other members of the Society for Psychical Research suggested he was a fraud), predictive messages, word-association tests, proxy sittings and book and newspaper tests. Detailed analysis of these sources, enabled Reverend Thomas to conclude he had ample justification to confirm that human personalities do survive bodily death.

By survival, he meant continuity of memory, of character, and of basic interests. He believed that surviving personalities retain vivid and detailed memories of their earth lives, and that they retain their basic attitudes and character traits. Furthermore, he believed that these surviving personalities, through Mrs Leonard, and through other competent mediums, have been able to converse with those whom they have left behind in earth life, and who seek such contacts.

Surviving personalities are also known as communicators, and they explained to Reverend Thomas that they were able to communicate through Mrs Leonard because of a 'power', which extended a few feet around her body. This would fade away towards the end of the sitting, meaning that communication was no longer possible.

This corresponds with today's understanding of 'opening up' and 'closing down' before and after a demonstration of mediumship. 'Opening up' allows the medium to throw out energy to connect with the Spirit World: effectively, opening the door to the Spirit World. 'Closing down' means shutting the door again. This causes communication to cease. Too much communication is tiring for the medium, and can cause illness and fatigue: and in some cases, nervous breakdowns.

Reverend Thomas' scientific integrity led to his election to the Council of the Society for Psychical Research. He served on it for nineteen years, and his membership in the Society extended over a period of more than half a century. Although he was a Spiritualist, this did not stop him from applying critical scientific methods when conducting research into survival of the spirit/soul (consciousness) after physical death.

CHAPTER FORTY-FIVE

James Hewat McKenzie

(1869-1929)

James Hewat McKenzie was a psychologist and psychoanalyst, but switched his attention to parapsychology: the study of psychic phenomena.

Psychical Research

He was born in Edinburgh. In 1900 he began to study the occult sciences, devoting much of his time to helping the development of spiritual mediums, such as Gladys Osborne Leonard (see Chapter 21) and Eileen Garrett (see Chapter 25). He became a Spiritualist, and spent a number of years touring, lecturing, and seeking out mediums to investigate. He travelled to the United States, the Middle East, Germany, Austria and Poland in order to do this.

His contributions to parapsychology, and its association with the Spiritualist Movement of the early twentieth century, can be considered his greatest legacy. It paved the way for the future study of clairvoyance and extrasensory perception (ESP).

ESP encompasses telepathy (reading the thoughts of others), precognition (sensing future events), psychokinesis (moving objects using the power of the mind), psychometry (reading the history of an object by touching it) and remote viewing (seeking impressions about a distant or unseen target: place, person, etc). In 1917 he wrote what is probably considered to be his main work, *Spirit Intercourse: Its Theory and Practice*.

Institute for Experimental Metaphysics

In April 1920, McKenzie and his wife founded the British College of Psychic Science in London. This was to promote the study of psychic and physical phenomena, and was very similar to the Institut Métapsychique International in Paris. In December 1938, the college merged with the International Institute for Psychical Research, becoming the Institute for Experimental Metaphysics. Unfortunately, during World War II, the Institute for Experimental Metaphysics closed, and in 1947 its library and records were destroyed.

Harry Houdini

In his book, *Spirit Intercourse: Its Theory and Practice*, McKenzie claimed the feats of the magician Harry Houdini were the result of psychic power, believing he had the power to materialise and dematerialise objects. Houdini, however, refuted this, saying that his abilities were the result of human strength and power, resting on natural laws of physics.

But was he telling the truth?

CHAPTER FORTY-SIX

Hereward Carrington

(1880-1958)

Hereward Carrington was a psychical researcher and member of the Society for Psychical Research.

Background

Hereward Carrington was born in St Helier, Jersey, and moved to the United States in 1888. In 1904, he settled in New York City, where he first worked as an assistant editor for *Street & Smith Publications*, which specialised in inexpensive paperbacks and magazines.

Psychical Research

Carrington started out as a sceptic, but his interest in psychic matters grew from reading books on the subject, and at the age of nineteen, he joined the London-based Society for Psychical Research.

In 1907, he went on to become a member of the American Society for Psychical Research, and worked for a year as assistant to the researcher, James Hyslop (see Chapter 41).

American Psychical Institute and Laboratory

In 1920, Carrington founded the American Psychical Institute and Laboratory for specialised research. The laboratory was one of the first to investigate physical phenomena.

He kept extensive records of his research and investigations, and in 1930 claimed that although he was not a Spiritualist, he was willing to grant that evidence supporting survival of the consciousness was strong.

Eileen Garrett

Carrington made a detailed study of the medium Eileen Garrett (see Chapter 25), who was one of the most talented trance mediums. Many entities spoke through her, and Carrington carried out a number of psychological tests to see if the 'beings' were secondary personalities, or, from the Spirit World. He described the results in his book: *The Case for Psychic Survival*, where he said that he believed the entities were independent personalities, with no strong emotional, or other connections with Garrett, or any portion of her subconscious.

Mysteries of Myra

Carrington was the primary consultant and contributor of story ideas for *The Mysteries of Myra*, a fifteen-episode silent film series released in 1916. The film introduced subjects such as automatic writing and astral projection (out-of-body experience) to the screen. The leading character, Dr Payson Alden, was the first paranormal investigator of the cinema, and was based on Carrington himself.

CHAPTER FORTY-SEVEN

Air Chief Marshall, Lord Hugh Dowding

(1882-1970)

Lord Dowding was an officer in the Royal Air Force during the Second World War and became a committed Spiritualist and researcher.

Background

Lord Dowding had a very distinguished career. He was born in Moffat, Dumfriesshire, the son of Arthur and Maud Dowding, and was educated at St Ninian's School, followed by Winchester College. He went on to train at the Royal Military Academy, Woolwich, and in 1900, was commissioned as a second lieutenant in the Royal Garrison Artillery. During the First World War (1914 – 1918), he served as a fighter pilot and a commander. During the Second World War, he was in charge of RAF Fighter Command.

Battle of Britain

When the Battle of Britain broke out in 1940, Lord Dowding played a crucial role in Britain's defence. This eventually countered Hitler's plan to invade Britain. It was a three-month campaign.

Lord Dowding was in charge of the young fighter pilots of Fighter Command. During the fighting he argued that Britain should not lose valuable fighter resources in the defence of France, and that they should be retained to defend Britain. Not everyone agreed, but eventually his tactics proved to be correct.

Hitler's Luftwaffe

The Luftwaffe was the German Air Force. Its aim was to destroy the Royal Air Force airfields and infrastructure in order to pave the way for an airborne invasion of Britain. Dowding developed a system involving new radar technology and rapid communications through a set of reporting chains, which monitored and led to the interception of Luftwaffe flights. It was the Battle of Britain's victory over Hitler's forces that led Winston Churchill to utter his memorable tribute: *'Never in the field of human conflict was so much owed by so many to so few.'* The brave young pilots, mostly British, but also from many other countries, were referred to by Churchill as Dowding's 'chicks' and eventually became known as 'The Few'.

Dowding was given a peerage in 1943 in recognition of his wartime services.

Spiritualism

When Lord Dowding retired as Commander-in-Chief of RAF Fighter Command, he began to wonder about the fate of the airmen who had sacrificed their lives in the battle. Did they still exist in another dimension, and if so, could they communicate with their loved ones?

This was a question many widows were also asking: amongst them Muriel Whiting, whose husband, Max, had died during a bombing mission over Eastern Europe. She was hoping to enlist Lord Dowding's help in finding out from the Air Ministry what had happened to him. Lord Dowding sent a letter of condolence to all those who wrote to him, but in Mrs Whiting's case, he extended an invitation to lunch to discuss Max's case.

When they met, Mrs Whiting asked Lord Dowding why he had invited her to lunch. Lord Dowding explained that shortly after receiving her letter, he had visited a medium, and Max had come through and said: *'I wish you would take my wife out to lunch. You will like her.'*

Lord Dowding, who was a widower, did like her. They fell in love and married. Muriel proved to be a great influence on his life. Dowding became increasingly occupied with spiritual matters, and with Spiritualism in particular. He recorded his quest for spiritual knowledge in a trilogy of books: *Many Mansions, Lychgate* and *Dark Star.* These books had a huge positive impact on a grieving world.

CHAPTER FORTY-EIGHT

Arthur Findlay

(1883-1964)

Arthur Findlay was a businessman who took a great interest in psychical research – and bequeathed Stansted Hall to the Spiritualists' National Union (SNU).

Background

Arthur Findlay was born in Glasgow. He was a writer, accountant, stockbroker and Justice of the Peace for the counties of Essex and Ayrshire. In 1913 he was awarded the title of 'Member of The Most Excellent Order of the British Empire' for his organisational work for the Red Cross. But it was his involvement in Spiritualism and psychical research that played the most significant part in his life.

Spiritualism and Psychical Research

At the age of seventeen, Findlay became interested in comparative religion. His parents were staunch Christians, and burned his collection of books to discourage his research. But this did not deter him. In 1918, he attended a séance with the direct voice medium, John Campbell Sloan (see Chapter 19). Findlay was so impressed with John's skills, that he spent the next five years investigating him, and wrote books about their experiences.

Books and Magazines

Findlay was a prolific writer and well-known speaker and lecturer. He was also one of the founders of the British Spiritualist periodical: *Psychic News*.

Organisations

Findlay founded various organisations, such as the Glasgow Society for Psychical Research and the International Institute for Psychical Research. He was an honorary member of the American Foundation for Psychical Research, and the Edinburgh Psychic College: now called the Edinburgh College of Parapsychology. He was also an honorary president of the Spiritualists' National Union.

Stansted Hall

Stansted Hall was built in 1871. In 1923 Findlay bought the estate, and on his death in 1964, the Hall, grounds and an endowment, were transferred to the Spiritualists' National Union. Stansted Hall is now known as the Arthur Findlay College. It offers excellent facilities as a residential centre where students can study spiritualist philosophy, healing and mediumship.

CHAPTER FORTY-NINE

Professor Archie Edmiston Roy

(1924-2012)

Archie Roy was a professor of Astronomy and founder of the Scottish Society for Psychical Research.

Background

Archie Roy was born in Clydebank, West Dunbartonshire, and educated at Hillhead High School, followed by the University of Glasgow. He went on to become Professor Emeritus of Astronomy at the University of Glasgow. Professor Roy was a Fellow of the Royal Society of Edinburgh, the Royal Astronomical Society, the British Interplanetary Society and the Scientific and Medical Network.

He was also elected a member of the European Academy of Arts, Sciences and the Humanities, where he worked with winners of great international prizes: their mission, to contribute to the maintenance of peace, by encouraging collaboration among nations in education, science, arts and humanities, without distinction of race, gender, language, religion, or political preference.

Psychical Research

Professor Roy was a member and past president of the Society for Psychical Research and founding president of the Scottish Society for Psychical Research. He investigated the paranormal for many years, often contributing to BBC Scotland television and radio discussions on the subject. From the late 1980s until 2010, he gave evening classes on the subject at Glasgow University's School of Physics and

Astronomy – and was nicknamed: the 'Glasgow Ghostbuster'.

His introduction to the Spirit World began in the 1950s after he lost his way in the old library at Glasgow University. He was most annoyed when he came upon shelves of books on Spiritualism and Psychical Research, until he recognised the names of some of the authors, which included Sir Oliver Lodge and Professor Sir William Crookes.

Professor Roy was often called in by the occupants of 'haunted' houses. One such case was poltergeist activity in a home in Maxwell Park, Glasgow. Before contacting him, the family had called the police, and one of the police officers later told him that he had to take some of his men off the case because they were submitting reports stating such things as:

> 'The bed was proceeding in a northerly direction...'

The problem was solved when Professor Roy and a church minister carried out a service of cleansing in each room of the house. This was an example of just one of the many cases dealt with by this remarkable man, throughout a career that spanned over fifty years.

The Glasgow Association of Spiritualists

CHAPTER FIFTY

The Glasgow Association of Spiritualists

We hope that the information in this book has given you some understanding of what Spiritualism is about. Mediums, healers, psychical researchers and churches of the past and present have all left their mark to some degree: so, let's not forget the pioneering role played by our own Church, which has faced many challenges during its lifetime.

The Glasgow Association of Spiritualists

On 22 January 1866, James Nicholson, a Glasgow writer and poet, joined forces with a well-known printer of that time: Hay Nisbet. Each signed a notice calling a meeting at the Buchanan Temperance Hotel in Glasgow. On 26 January 1866, the Glasgow Association of Spiritualists (GAS) was created.

It has been widely reported that the first president was Andrew Glendinning. Mr Glendinning was certainly integral to the early development of GAS, but recent research has revealed that he was never, in fact, president. The first president is believed to have been a gentleman called James Marshall, but this still has to be confirmed. To-date, not much is known about him, but an investigation into the facts is currently being carried out by the committee of the Glasgow Association of Spiritualists.

Hay Nisbet would become GAS's fourth president in 1872 and he would go on to introduce the *Spiritual Record*, which started out as a monthly magazine, then owing to its popularity, would become a weekly.

During this time, Mesmerism was also becoming popular. Some of the Mesmerists went on to join the Glasgow Association of Spiritualists, and in 1873, GAS began to issue its first healing reports to members. Also that year, GAS formed its own Children's Lyceum, however, regular Sunday meetings did not take place until 1 April 1888.

The Lyceum was a school of liberal and harmonious education. The educational methods used were aimed at drawing the inherent qualities of the individual, rather than imparting knowledge that may be obtained elsewhere. Self-expression and musical and artistic talents were encouraged, and harmony was the keynote of all activities. As time moved on, the Lyceum would provide education and training of an advanced and liberal nature to Spiritualists of all ages.

In 1914, World War I broke out. Everyone suffered the loss of someone. Young soldiers were crossing to the Spirit World. They were eager to make contact with their families in the physical world, and their families needed to know if they were safe, so interest in Spiritualism intensified.

From its conception, GAS had moved around from one rented property to another. A building fund was set up, but it took until 1919, for it to accumulate sufficient funds to buy two houses in Holland Street (Glasgow). Plans were put in place to build a church hall (James Robertson Hall) to accommodate six hundred people. On 23 June 1923 the Hall was opened.

Interest in Spiritualism continued to grow. In 1939 GAS purchased the 'Greek' Thomson Church in St Vincent Street (Glasgow), which was designed by the architect, Alexander Thomson. The Church, which became the most impressive headquarters of any Spiritualist organisation, cost £4,250 to buy, and had a seating capacity of one thousand five hundred. On 1 September 1939, World War II broke out. On 19 November 1939, GAS moved into its new premises.

As war raged throughout Europe, people flocked to the Church in the hope of making contact with their loved ones, who had died in the fighting. The war ended in 1945, but attendances remained high. Unfortunately, as time progressed, attendances began to decline. Then, just as they started to show signs of increasing again, GAS was faced with another unexpected problem: compulsory purchase.

In 1964, Glasgow Corporation took over the 'Greek' Thomson Church by compulsory purchase. The Corporation wanted to restore and preserve the building because of its architectural importance to the City of Glasgow. GAS was faced with a choice: rent the Church, or move. GAS decided to rent the Church for a while, until it located new premises.

In 1970, GAS purchased two large Victorian terrace houses: 6 and 7 Somerset Place (Glasgow). A hall was built on the ground at the rear, and on 19 December 1970 the new premises were opened to the public. Somerset Place remained the home of GAS, but church attendances fluctuated. Then in 2020, GAS was confronted with another unexpected problem: all churches, whatever their denomination, had to shut their doors to the public – the reason: Covid-19.

By March 2020, the world was in lockdown. It was unknown how long this would last, but as the weeks went by, GAS decided it had to do something. It had to turn this unexpected negative situation into a positive one. The joiner and decorator were called in and did their stuff. In September 2020, the electrician was called in to install LED light fittings. All was going well: until disaster! The electrician wasn't happy with the state of the electrics. He condemned the first floor at number 6, and rewired it in order to bring it up to proper safety standards. Then the rest of the electrics were failed, which meant that the entire premises needed to be rewired: a matter that would have to be put to the church members for further consideration.

In October 2020 it was agreed to open the doors to members for one day to hold an AGM. The SNU stepped in to assist. Concerns were raised about dampness in the buildings. Members agreed that work had to be done, but motions still had to be put in place. The SNU advised that in order to comply with the rules, GAS had to obtain three separate quotes for each large job: and contractors had to be reputable and insured.

Fortunately, Covid restrictions did not prohibit the building industry. Contractors continued to work. By February 2021, GAS was in the process of rounding up contractors to tackle the dampness. Most were daunted by the size of the job, which was to deal with a combination of dry rot and rising damp. By May 2021, GAS had submitted its three quotes for the treatment of dampness in the basement area. The SNU approved GAS's choice of contractor, but added that under normal circumstances members' approval would be needed before work could be carried out. However, given the Covid situation, and the unlikelihood of another general meeting being called any time soon, the SNU granted GAS dispensation to proceed, on the understanding it would seek members' retrospective approval at the earliest possible opportunity.

By July 2021, Covid restrictions in Glasgow were at level 3. From a legal perspective GAS was allowed to open its doors to the public, whilst observing all the necessary rules that included hygiene and social distancing. But the basement was in a mess: and that was where the toilets were. Not only that, the premises couldn't be properly cleaned, and there was the added issue of the electrics. Finally, there was a concern that there might be asbestos within the floors that were being treated. It was decided that in the interest of Health and Safety the church had to remain shut.

The asbestos specialists stepped in to do an asbestos survey. They couldn't get through all the additional samples from the floors in one day, so had to come back a couple of weeks later. Finally, the report was ready. The additional samples proved negative for asbestos, but the report expressed its concerns about the asbestos in the boiler room, giving a quote for an environmental clean-up of the boiler flues and the boiler room floor.

Then, yet another unexpected disaster: the water tank in the flat on the top floor of number 7 sprang a leak. Emergency steps were taken to empty it and make sure it didn't fill again. The plumbers came out and advised that since the water tank was made of fibreglass, it could not be repaired. The pipes would have to be re-routed to the water tank in the boiler room. Unfortunately, to get hot water, the water tank in the boiler room would have to be replaced, but before work could be done in the boiler room, the asbestos would have to be cleared.

GAS was scratching its head. The old boilers were on their last legs, but hadn't yet been termed an emergency. The asbestos company had already given a quote for an environmental clean-up of the boiler flues and the boiler room floor, but then so too had another company, long before lockdown: only their quote covered the removal of the flues and replacement of the boilers. Why pay for the treatment of the flues, if they would ultimately be removed? The boilers had just become a priority. Arrangements were made to install a new efficient boiler and hot water solution: and the basement cast iron radiators were sent for reconditioning.

Then it was time to tidy up. The plasterer filled in the holes made by the electricians in every room. Volunteers stepped in to paint. Floors were laminated and carpeted. By September 2022, the operation was almost complete, sufficiently so, to invite the public back in. On 4 September 2022, the doors opened and the congregation returned, enabling GAS to take its first tentative steps towards becoming a new progressive establishment.

The Phoenix rises from the ashes!

The Glasgow Association of Spiritualists is proud to say that it has overcome many challenges, and continues to grow. We invite you to visit our church in Glasgow, and take a gentle stroll round the many galleries depicting the lives and struggles of our brave pioneers.

However, you should remember that these are pioneers of the past. We are now looking to the future, and we hope that by learning from them, you will develop with us, and embrace every opportunity to become Spiritualism's next generation of pioneers.

Stories of the Pioneers 163

A temporary glitch!

In April 2024, an external downpipe 'gave up the ghost', and flooded parts of the premises. GAS closed again. Internal damage resulted: some ceilings collapsed and some of the new laminate and carpeting was damaged. Contractors came out and volunteers went into action. However, during this period, grants were obtained to help fund the replacement of two irreparable roofs: and a grand job has been done. At the time of writing, internal repairs are ongoing, but GAS will have its doors back open to the public in September 2024.

We look forward to seeing you all!

Caroline A Scott
President
The Glasgow Association of Spiritualists
August 2024

New Roofs!

Bibliography

Early History of Spiritual and Psychic Phenomena

Glasgow Association of Spiritualists: An Outline and History, by Glasgow Association of Spiritualists.
Spirit of the New Millennium: The Ultimate Theory, by Frank Newman.
Multiple Universes and Religion, by Frank Newman.
Natural and Supernatural: A History of the Paranormal from the Earliest Times to 1914, by Brian Inglis.
Spirits of the Earth: A Guide to Native American Nature Symbols, Stories and Ceremonies, by Bobby Lake-Thom
The Cherokee Herbal: Native Plant Medicine from the Four Directions, by J.T. Garrett.
Earth Quest - Earth Medicine: Revealing Hidden Treasures of the Native American Medicine Wheel - a Shamanic Way to Self-discovery, by Kenneth Meadows.
Mother Earth Spirituality: Native American Paths to Healing Ourselves and Our World, by Ed McGaa.
The Soul of the Indian, by Charles Alexander Eastman.
Bone Medicine: A Native American Shaman's Guide to Physical Wholeness, by Wolf Moondance.
Wolf Medicine: A Native American Shamanic Journey into the Mind, by Wolf Moondance.
Rainbow Spirit Journeys: Native American Meditations Dreams, by Wolf Moondance.
Vision Quest: Native American Magical Healing, by Wolf Moondance.
Spirit Medicine: Native American Teachings to Awaken the Spirit, by Wolf Moondance.
Earth Magic: Ancient Shamanic Wisdom for Healing Yourself, Others, and the Planet, by Steven D. Farmer.

The World We Used to Live In: Remembering the Powers of the Medicine Men, by Vine Deloria Jr.
Old Souls: The Sages and Mystics of Our World, by Aletheia Luna.
The Wisdom of the Native Americans: Including the Soul of an Indian and Other Writings of Ohiyesa and the Great Speeches of Red Jacket, Chief Joseph, and Chief Seattle, by Kent Nerburn.
Faces of Your Soul: Rituals in Art, Mask Making, and Guided Imagery with Ancestors, Spirit Guides, and Totem Animals, by Kaleo Ching.
Animal Spirit Guides: An Easy-to-Use Handbook for Identifying and Understanding Your Power Animals and Animal Spirit Helpers, by Steven D. Farmer.
Sacred Plant Medicine: The Wisdom in Native American Herbalism, by Stephen Harrod Buhner.
The Spiritual Technology of Ancient Egypt: Sacred Science and the Mystery of Consciousness, by Edward F. Malkowski.
The Sacred Magic of Ancient Egypt: The Spiritual Practice Restored, by Rosemary Clark.
Religion and Ritual in Ancient Egypt, by Emily Teeter.
Temple of the Cosmos: The Ancient Egyptian Experience of the Sacred, by Jeremy Naydler.
God and the ancient Chinese, by Samuel Wang.
Tao: The Watercourse Way, by Alan W. Watts.
Greek Oracles, by H.W. Parke.
Girls and Women in Classical Greek Religion, by Matthew Dillon.
The Ancient Oracles: Making the Gods Speak, by Richard Stoneman.
The Sibylline Oracles: Translated from the Greek into English Blank Verse, by Milton S. Terry (Translator).
Life of the Great Mahasiddha Virupa, by D.Kalden & D. Sakya.
Scottish Folklore, by Raymond Lamont-Brown.
Little Book of Scottish Folklore, by Joules and Ken Taylor.
Scottish Legends and Folklore, by Ian McGregor.
Haunted Castles & Houses of Scotland, by Martin Coventry.
The Haunted: A Social History of Ghosts, by Owen Davies.
The Brahan Seer: The Making of a Legend, by Alex Sutherland.

Witchcraft v Mediumship

Witchcraft and Magic in Europe, Volume 1: Biblical and Pagan Societies, by Bengt Ankarloo.
Witchcraft and Magic in Europe, Volume 2: Ancient Greece and Rome, by Bengt Ankarloo.
Witchcraft and Magic in Europe, Volume 3: The Middle-Ages, by Bengt Ankarloo.
Witchcraft and Magic in Europe, Volume 4: The Period of the Witch Trials, by Bengt Ankarloo.
Witchcraft and Magic in Europe, Volume 6: The Twentieth Century, by Bengt Ankarloo.
Witchcraft in Europe and the New World, 1400-1800, by P.G. Maxwell-Stuart.
Witch Hunters, by P.G. Maxwell-Stuart.
Beyond the Witch Trials: Witchcraft and Magic in Enlightenment Europe, by Owen Davies.
Witchcraft, Magic and Culture, 1736-1951, by Owen Davies.
Salem Possessed: The Social Origins of Witchcraft, by Paul S. Boyer.
Accused: British Witches throughout History, by Willow Winsham.
Witchcraft: A Very Short Introduction, by Malcolm Gaskill.
Witchfinders, by Malcolm Gaskill.
Joan of Arc, by Mark Twain.
Joan: The Mysterious Life of the Heretic Who Became a Saint, by Donald Spoto.
Voices: The Final Hours of Joan of Arc, by David Elliott.
Clairaudience: My Perceived Disability, by Chigozie Ugwueze.
Clairvoyance and Clairaudience, by Annie Besant.
Nostradamus: The Complete Prophecies for the Future, by Mario Reading.
Prophecies of Nostradamus, by Nostradamus.
Hellish Nell: Last of Britain's Witches, by Malcolm Gaskill.
The Two Worlds of Helen Duncan, by Gena Brealey.
The Strange Case of Hellish Nell: The Story of Helen Duncan and the Witch Trial of World War II, by Nina Shandler.
The Trial of Mrs Duncan, by C.E. Bechhofer Roberts.

Taking Up the Challenge, by Eric Hatton.
The Fall of the House of Skeptics: Science and Psychic Phenomena, by Chris Carter.
Science and the Afterlife Experience: Evidence for the Immortality of Consciousness, by Chris Carter.

Emanuel Swedenborg

Heaven and Hell, by Emanuel Swedenborg.
Afterlife: A Guided Tour to Heaven and Its Wonders, by Emanuel Swedenborg.
Divine Love and Wisdom, by Emanuel Swedenborg.
Divine Providence, by Emanuel Swedenborg.
Journal of Dreams, by Emanuel Swedenborg.
Arcana Coelestia. The Heavenly Arcana Contained in the Holy Scriptures or Word of the Lord Unfolded Beginning with the Book of Genesis, by Emanuel Swedenborg.
Life on Other Planets, by Emanuel Swedenborg.
Spiritual Life and the Word of God, by Emanuel Swedenborg.
Earths in Our Solar System Which Are Called Planets and Earths in the Starry Heaven Their Inhabitants and the Spirits and Angels There, by Emanuel Swedenborg.
Our Life after Death: A First-hand Account from an 18th-Century Scientist and Seer, by Emanuel Swedenborg.
The Lives of Angels, by Emanuel Swedenborg.
Angelic Wisdom about Divine Providence, by Emanuel Swedenborg.
The Heavenly City: A Spiritual Guidebook, by Emanuel Swedenborg.
Regeneration: Spiritual Growth and How It Works, by Emanuel Swedenborg.

Andrew Jackson Davis

The Magic Staff: An Autobiography of Andrew Jackson Davis, by Andrew Jackson Davis.

Beyond the Valley: A Sequel to the Magic Staff: An Autobiography of Andrew Jackson Davis, by Andrew Jackson Davis.
The History and Philosophy of Evil, by Andrew Jackson Davis.
The Harmonial Philosophy: a compendium and digest of the works of Andrew Jackson Davis, the seer of Poughkeepsie, by Andrew Jackson Davis.
The Principles of Nature, Her Divine Revelations, by Andrew Jackson Davis.
Death and the Afterlife, by Andrew Jackson Davis.
A Stellar Key to the Summer Land, by Andrew Jackson Davis.
Views of Our Heavenly Home - A Sequel to a Stellar Key to the Summer-Land, by Andrew Jackson Davis.
The Diakka, and Their Earthly Victims, by Andrew Jackson Davis.
The Harmonial Philosophy and Death and the After Life, by Andrew Jackson Davis.
The Great Harmonia; Being a Philosophical Revelation of the Natural, Spiritual, and Celestial Universe, Vol. 1, by Andrew Jackson Davis.
The Great Harmonia: Being a Philosophical Revelation of the Natural, Spiritual, and Celestial Universe, Volume 2, by Andrew Jackson Davis.
Events in the Life of a Seer: Being a Memoranda of Authentic Facts in Magnetism, Clairvoyance, Spiritualism, by Andrew Jackson Davis.
Memoranda of Persons, Places, and Events; Embracing Authentic Facts, Visions, Impressions, Discoveries, in Magnetism, Clairvoyance, Spiritualism, by Andrew Jackson Davis.

Margaret and Kate Fox

Talking to the Dead: Kate and Maggie Fox and the Rise of Spiritualism, by Barbara Weisberg.
Arctic Explorations, by Elisha Kent Kane.
*The Love-Life of Dr. Kane: Containing the Correspondence, and a History of the Acquaintance, Engagement, and Secret

Marriage between Elisha K. Kane and Margaret Fox, by Elisha Kent Kane.
Exploring Other Worlds: Margaret Fox, Elisha Kent Kane, and the Antebellum Culture of Curiosity, by David Chapin.
Phenomena of Materialisation: A Contribution to the Investigation of Mediumistic Teleplastics, by Albert Freiherr Von Schrenck-Notzing.
Phenomena of Materialisation, by Albert Freiherr Von Schrenck-Notzing.
Life after Death: Some of the Best Evidence, by Jan W. Vandersande.
How to Do Automatic Writing, by Edain McCoy.
How to Do Automatic Writing, by Kuriakos.
Parapsychology: A Beginner's Guide, by Caroline Watt.
Parapsychology, by Richard Wiseman.
Levitation, by Steve Richards.

Robert Owen

A New View of Society, by Robert Owen.
Robert Owen on Education, by Robert Owen.
The Revolution in the Mind and Practice of the Human Race: Or, the Coming Change from Irrationality to Rationality, by Robert Owen.

Emma Hardinge Britten

Art Magic: Or Mundane, Sub Mundane, and Super Mundane Spiritism, by Emma Hardinge Britten.
Ghost Land: Researches into the Mysteries of Occultism, by Emma Hardinge Britten.
Autobiography of Emma Hardinge Britten, by Emma Hardinge Britten.
Modern American Spiritualism: A Twenty Years' Record of the Communion between Earth and the World of Spirits, by Emma Hardinge Britten.
Nineteenth century miracles; or, Spirits and their work in every country of the earth. A complete historical compendium of the

great movement known as modern spiritualism, by Emma Hardinge Britten.
The Wildfire Club: And Other Stories, by Emma Hardinge Britten.
Spiritualism in America, by Emma Hardinge Britten.
Spiritualism in Great Britain, by Emma Hardinge Britten.
Spiritualism in Australia, by Emma Hardinge Britten.
Spiritualism in Germany, by Emma Hardinge Britten.
Spiritualism in Russia, by Emma Hardinge Britten.
Nineteenth Century Miracles; or, Spirits and Their Work in Every Country of the Earth. A Complete Historical Compendium of the Great Movement known as Modern Spiritualism, by Emma Hardinge Britten.
A Noble Pioneer: The Life Story of Emma Hardinge Britten, by James Robertson.
The Key to Theosophy, by Helena Petrovna Blavatsky.
The Other World: Spiritualism and Psychical Research in England, by Janet Oppenheim.
Other Powers: The Age of Suffrage, Spiritualism, and the Scandalous Victoria Woodhull, by Barbara Goldsmith.
The Philosophy of Spiritualism, by Carole Austin.
Just Ask the Universe: A No-Nonsense Guide to Manifesting Your Dreams, by Michael Samuels.
Keep Calm and Ask On: A No-Nonsense Guide to Fulfilling Your Dreams, by Michael Samuels.
E-Squared: Nine Do-It-Yourself Energy Experiments That Prove Your Thoughts Create Your Reality, by Pam Grout.
The Power of Spiritual Thought: "You Are What You Think", by Frederick Ormonde Murph.
The Wisdom of Your Cells: How Your Beliefs Control Your Biology, by Bruce H. Lipton.
Hands of Light: A Guide to Healing Through the Human Energy Field, by Barbara Ann Brennan.
Intuitive Studies: A Complete Course in Mediumship, by Gordon Smith.
Developing Mediumship, by Gordon Smith.
Where Two Worlds Meet, by Janet Nohavec.
The Spirits' Book, by Allan Kardec.

Ira and William Davenport

A Biography of the Brothers Davenport, London, by T. L. Nichols.
Spiritual Experiences, Including Seven Months with the Brothers Davenport, by Robert Cooper.

William and Horatio Eddy

The physical phenomena of Spiritualism, by Hereward Carrington.
People from the Other World, by Henry Steel Olcott.

David Duguid

Hafed, Prince of Persia, by Hay Nisbet.
Hermes, a Disciple of Jesus: His Life and Missionary Work; Also, the Evangelistic Travels of Anah and Zitha, together with Incidents in the Life of Jesus, Spirit Communications Received Through D. Duguid, by Hay Nisbet.
The Case for Spirit Photography, by Arthur Conan Doyle.
The Veil Lifted: Modern Developments of Spirit Photography, by J T Taylor, A Glendinning and J Robertson.
Photographing the Invisible, by James Coates.
Seeing the Invisible, by James Coates.
Mediums and the Spiritual Press: A Protest, by James Coates.
Human Magnetism: How to Hypnotise, by James Coates.
How to Thought Read, by James Coates.
Spiritualism: The Open Door to the Unseen Universe, by James Robertson.

Daniel Dunglas Home

Incidents in My Life, by Daniel Dunglas Home.
D D Home: His Life His Mission, by Madam Home.
Lights and Shadows of Spiritualism, by Daniel Dunglas Home.
Spiritualism, by John W Edmonds.
The Martyrs of Science, by Sir David Brewster.
Letters on Natural Magic Addressed to Sir Walter Scott, Bart, by Sir David Brewster.
More Worlds than One: The Creed of the Philosopher and the Hope of the Christian, by Sir David Brewster.

Reverend William Stainton Moses

Spirit Teachings: Through the Mediumship of William Stainton Moses, by William Stainton Moses.
More Spirit Teachings: Further Examples of Remarkable Communication from Beyond, by William Stainton Moses.
Direct Writing by Supernormal Means: A Record of Evidence for Spirit-Action, in the Manner before Called "Psychography", by William Stainton Moses.
Ghostly Visitors: A Series of Authentic Narratives, by William Stainton Moses.
Spirit-Identity, by William Stainton Moses.
Higher Aspects of Spiritualism, by (M.A., Oxon) William Stainton Moses.
The Ghost Club: Newly Found Tales of Victorian Terror, by William Meikle.
Complete Ghost Stories, by Charles Dickens.
The Controls of Stainton Moses, by A W Trethewy.

Madame d'Esperance

Shadow Land: Or, Light from the Other Side, by Elizabeth d'Esperance.
What I Know of Materialisations: From Personal Experience, by Elizabeth d'Esperance.
Northern Lights and Other Psychic Stories, by Elizabeth d'Esperance.
The Philosophy of Spirit, by William Oxley.

Angelic Revelations: Concerning the Origin, Ultimation and Destiny of the Human Spirit, by William Oxley.
William Oxley: His Life and Times from a Spiritual Standpoint, by William Oxley.

Florence Cook

The Spiritualists: The Story of Florence Cook and William Crookes, by Trevor H. Hall.

Leonora Piper

Resurrecting Leonora Piper: How Science Discovered the Afterlife, by Michael Tymn.

Reverend George Vale Owen

The Highlands of Heaven, by Rev George Vale Owen.
The Lowlands of Heaven, by Rev George Vale Owen.
The Ministry of Heaven, by Rev George Vale Owen.
The Outlands of Heaven, by Rev George Vale Owen.
The Battalions of Heaven, by Rev George Vale Owen.

John Sloan

On the Edge of the Etheric: Survival after Death Scientifically Explained, by Arthur Findlay.
Where Two Worlds Meet, by Arthur Findlay.

Edgar Cayce

Edgar Cayce on Atlantis, by Edgar Cayce.
Edgar Cayce on the Power of Colour, Stones, and Crystals, by Edgar Cayce.
Auras, by Edgar Cayce.
Reincarnation & Karma, by Edgar Cayce.

You Can Remember Your Past Lives, by Edgar Cayce.
Channelling Your Higher Self, by Edgar Cayce.
The Power of Your Mind, by Edgar Cayce.
Edgar Cayce on the Akashic Records, by Kevin J. Todeschi.

Gladys Osborne Leonard

My Life in Two Worlds, by Gladys Osborne Leonard.
The Last Crossing, by Gladys Osborne Leonard.

Rebecca Beard

Everyman's Search, by Rebecca Beard.
Everyman's Goal, by Rebecca Beard.

Frank Leah

Faces of the Living Dead, by Paul Miller.

Estelle Roberts

Fifty Years a Medium: The Autobiography of Estelle Roberts, by Estelle Roberts.
Red Cloud, the Control of Mrs Estelle Roberts: The Teachings of Red Cloud 1934 - Red Cloud's Lectures 1930-1932, by Estelle Roberts.
Red Cloud Speaks - My mission, by Estelle Roberts.
Red Cloud Speaks: Trance Teachings through Estelle Roberts, by Estelle Roberts.
Be DEAR to Yourself, by Estelle Roberts.

Eileen Garrett

Many Voices: The Autobiography of a Medium, by Eileen J. Garrett.

Adventures in the Supernormal, by Eileen Garrett.
Eileen Garrett and the world beyond the senses, by Allan Angoff.
Eileen Garrett Returns, by Robert Leichtman.

Grace Cooke

Wisdom from White Eagle, by Grace Cooke.
Arthur Conan Doyle's Book of the Beyond, by Colum Hayward, Grace Cooke.
Memories of Reincarnation, by Grace Cooke.

Harry Edwards

Guide for the Development of Mediumship, by Harry Edwards.
A Guide to the Understanding and Practice of Spiritual Healing, by Harry Edwards.
Spirit Healing, by Harry Edwards.
The Healing Intelligence, by Harry Edwards.
Psychic Healing, by Harry Edwards.
Harry Edwards: Thirty Years a Spiritual Healer, by Harry Edwards.
Life in Spirit: with a Guide for the Development of Mediumship, by Harry Edwards.

Anthony Borgia

Facts, by Anthony Borgia.
The World Unseen (Life on Other Worlds), by Anthony Borgia.
Life in the World Unseen, by Anthony Borgia.
More about Life in the World Unseen, by Anthony Borgia.
Here and Hereafter, by Anthony Borgia.

Maurice Barbanell

This is Spiritualism, by Maurice Barbanell.
Philosophy of Silver Birch, by Maurice Barbanell.

Silver Birch Speaks, by Maurice Barbanell.
The Barbanell Report, by Maurice Barbanell.
Power of the Spirit, by Maurice Barbanell.
Spiritualism Today, by Maurice Barbanell.
Where There's a Will, by Maurice Barbanell.
Harry Edwards and his Healing, by Maurice Barbanell.
Saga of Spirit Healing, by Maurice Barbanell.
When a Child Dies, by Sylvia Barbanell.
When Your Animal Dies, by Sylvia Barbanell.

Leslie Flint

Voices in the Dark: My Life as a Medium, by Leslie Flint.

Albert Best

Beyond Reasonable Doubt: the case for supernatural phenomena in the modern world, by Gordon Smith.
Best of Both Worlds: A Tribute to a Great Medium, by Archie Roy.

Gordon Higginson

On the Side of Angels, by Gordon Higginson.

Alfred Russel Wallace

Darwinism, by Alfred Russel Wallace.
Is Mars Habitable? A Critical Examination of Professor Percival Lowell's Book Mars and its Canals, with an Alternative Explanation, by Alfred Russel Wallace.
The Works of Alfred Russel Wallace, by Alfred Russel Wallace.
Contributions to the Theory of Natural Selection A Series of Essays, by Alfred Russel Wallace.
My Life: A Record of Events and Opinion, by Alfred Russel Wallace.

On the Tendency of Varieties to Depart Indefinitely From the Original Type, by Alfred Russel Wallace.
Man's Place in the Universe: A Study of the Results of Scientific Research In Relation To the Unity or Plurality of Worlds, by Alfred Russel Wallace.
The Wonderful Century: its Successes & Failures, by Alfred Russel Wallace.
Miracles and Modern Spiritualism, by Alfred Russel Wallace.

Sir William Crookes

Researches in the Phenomena of Spiritualism, by William Crookes.
Crookes and the spirit world, by William Crookes.
Remarkable Spirit Manifestations, by William Crookes.
The Chemical News and Journal of Industrial Science, by William Crookes.

Henry Sidgwick

The Methods of Ethics, by Henry Sidgwick.
Outlines of the History of Ethics for English Readers, by Henry Sidgwick.
Practical Ethics: Collection of Addresses and Essays, by Henry Sidgwick.
Henry Sidgwick: A Memoir, by Henry Sidgwick.
The Elements of Politics, by Henry Sidgwick.
Philosophy, its scope and relations; an introductory course of lectures, by Henry Sidgwick.
Presidential Addresses to the Society for Psychical Research, by Henry Sidgwick.
The Progress of the Women's Suffrage Movement, by Eleanor Mildred Sidgwick.
Phantasms of the Living: Cases of Telepathy Printed in the Journal of the Society for Psychical Research during Thirty-Five Years, by Eleanor Mildred Sidgwick.
Henry Sidgwick, by Eleanor Mildred Sidgwick.

University Education for Women: Presidential Address Delivered to the Education Society, Manchester University, on 21st November, 1912, by Eleanor Mildred Sidgwick.

Frederick Myers

Human Personality and Its Survival of Bodily Death, by F. W. H. Myers.
Science and a Future Life: With Other Essays (1893), by Frederick Myers.
Human Personality and Its Survival of Bodily Death: Volume 1 (1903), by Frederick Myers.
Human Personality and Its Survival of Bodily Death: Volume 2 (1903, by Frederick Myers.

William Barrett

Deathbed Visions, by William Fletcher Barrett.
On the Threshold of the Unseen: an examination of the phenomena of Spiritualism and of the evidence for survival after death, by Sir William F. Barrett.
The Divining Rod: An Experimental and Psychological Investigation, by William Fletcher Barrett.
Visual Hallucinations and Phantasms of the Living and Dead, by William Fletcher Barrett.
Psychical Research and the Threshold of the Unseen, by William Fletcher Barrett.
Psychical Research, by William Fletcher Barrett.
On the Threshold of a New World of Thought an Examination of the Phenomena of Spiritualism, by William Fletcher Barrett.
Practical Physics; an Introductory Handbook for the Physical Laboratory, by William Fletcher Barrett.
The Credibility of Dowsing, by William Fletcher Barrett.
Personality Survives Death: After-Death Communication from Sir William Barrett, by Florence Elizabeth Barrett.

Edmund Gurney

The Power of Sound, by Edmund Gurney.
Phantasms of the Living (History of Psychiatry), by Edmund Gurney.
Proceedings, Volume 1, by Edmund Gurney.
Society for Psychical Research (Great Britain), by Edmund Gurney.
Tertium Quid: The Human Ideal. 'Natural Religion.' the Controversy of Life. A Chapter in the Ethics of Pain. An Epilogue on Vivisection. The Nature of Evidence in Matters Extraordinary. The Utilitarian 'Ought.' Monism, by Edmund Gurney.

Charles Richet

Idiot Man, or the Follies of Mankind ("L'Homme Stupide"), by Charles Richet.
Thirty Years of Psychical Research, by Charles Richet.
Peace and War, by Charles Richet.
Physiology and Histology of the Cerebral Convolutions. Also, Poisons of the Intellect, by Charles Richet.
The Natural History of a Savant, by Charles Richet.

Sir Oliver Lodge

Pioneers of Science, by Oliver Lodge.
Raymond or Life and Death: With Examples of the Evidence for Survival of Memory and Affection after Death, by Oliver Lodge.
The Ether of Space, by Oliver Lodge.
Modern Problems, by Oliver Lodge.
The Immortality of the Soul, by Oliver Lodge.
Why I Believe in Personal Immortality, by Oliver Lodge.
The Proofs of Life after Death, by Oliver Lodge.
Life and Matter a Criticism of Professor Haeckel's 'Riddle of the Universe', by Oliver Lodge.
Signalling Across Space without Wires: Being a Description of the Work of Hertz & His Successors, by Oliver Lodge.
Past Years: an Autobiography, by Oliver Lodge.

James H Hyslop

Psychical Research and the Resurrection, by James H Hyslop.
Problems of philosophy; or principles of epistemology and metaphysics, by James H Hyslop.
Borderland of Psychical Research, by James H. Hyslop.

Sir Arthur Conan Doyle

The History of Spiritualism, by Arthur Conan Doyle.
The Wanderings of a Spiritualist, by Sir Arthur Conan Doyle.
The New Revelation, by Arthur Conan Doyle.
Those Who Haunt Ghosts: A Century of Ghost Hunter Fiction, by Arthur Conan Doyle, Henry James, J.H. Riddell, Ambrose Bierce, H.G. Wells, Rudyard Kipling, Algernon Blackwood, W.W. Jacobs.
Conan Doyle and the Mysterious World of Light, by Matt Wingett.
Arthur and me: the true story of Arthur Conan Doyle communicating from beyond the grave, by Ann Treherne.
The Edge of the Unknown, by Arthur Conan Doyle.

Gustav Geley

From the Unconscious to the Conscious, by Gustav Geley.
Clairvoyance and Materialization: A Record of Experiments, by Gustav Geley.
Reincarnation, by Gustav Geley.

Reverend Charles Drayton Thomas

Some New Evidence for Human Survival, by Charles Drayton Thomas.
Life beyond Death with Evidence, by Charles Drayton Thomas.
From Life to Life: A Story of Family Reunion after Death, by Charles Drayton Thomas.

James Hewat McKenzie

Spirit Intercourse: Its Theory and Practice, by J. Hewat McKenzie.

Hereward Carrington

Your Psychic Powers and How to Develop Them, by Hereward Carrington.
True Ghost Stories, by Hereward Carrington.
The Problems of Psychical Research: Experiments and Theories in the Realm of the Supernormal, by Hereward Carrington.
Haunted People: The Story of the Poltergeist down the Centuries, by Hereward Carrington.
Haunted Houses: Their Theory and Cure, by Hereward Carrington.
The Phantom Armies Seen in France, by Hereward Carrington.
The American Séances with Eusapia Palladino, by Hereward Carrington.
The Invisible Hand - True Ghost Stories, by Hereward Carrington.
The Kundalini's Secret Energy and how it is aroused, by Hereward Carrington.
Clairvoyance, by Hereward Carrington.
Keys to the Occult: Two Guides to Hidden Wisdom, by Hereward Carrington.
Loaves and Fishes; a Study of the Miracles, of the Resurrection, and of the Future Life in the Light of Modern Psychic Knowledge, by Hereward Carrington.
The World of Psychic Research, by Hereward Carrington.
The Mental Phenomenon of Psychic Science, by Hereward Carrington.
The Physical Phenomenon of Psychic Science, by Hereward Carrington.
The Classic Secrets of Magic & Escapology, by Hereward Carrington.
Matter through Matter, by Hereward Carrington.

Laboratory Investigations into Psychic Phenomena, by Hereward Carrington.
Essays in the Occult, by Hereward Carrington.
The Coming Science, by Hereward Carrington.
Ouija Board and Automatic Writing – Annotated by Hereward Carrington.
The Phenomena of Astral Projection, by Hereward Carrington.
How to Project the Astral Body, by Hereward Carrington.
Death, its Causes and Phenomena, by Hereward Carrington.
Nature's Law of Cure, by Hereward Carrington.
The Seven Wonders of the World; Atlantis, the Lost Continent; Islands of Mystery, Historic Facts about Real and Phantom Islands, by Hereward Carrington.
Higher Psychical Development (Yoga Philosophy), by Hereward Carrington.
Genuine Spiritualism and Psychic Phenomena, by Hereward Carrington.
Your Memory: How to Improve It, by Hereward Carrington.
Story of Psychic Science, by Hereward Carrington.
Psychical phenomena and the war, by Hereward Carrington.
Modern Psychical Phenomena, Recent Researches and Speculations, by Hereward Carrington.
Mental Telepathy Explained, by Hereward Carrington.
Houdini and Conan Doyle: The Story of a Strange Friendship, by Bernard M.L. Ernst and Hereward Carrington.

Air Chief Marshall, Lord Hugh Dowding

Many Mansions, by Lord Dowding.
God's Magic, by Lord Dowding.
Lychgate: The Entrance to the Path, by Lord Dowding.
The Dark Star, by Lord Dowding.
A Summer Bright and Terrible: Winston Churchill, Lord Dowding, Radar, and the Impossible Triumph of the Battle of Britain, by David E. Fisher.
In Times of War: Messages of Wisdom from Soldiers in the Afterlife, by Jonathan Beecher.

Arthur Findlay

On the Edge of the Etheric: Survival after Death Scientifically Explained, by Arthur Findlay.
The Curse of Ignorance: a History of Mankind, by Arthur Findlay.
The Rock of Truth or Spiritualism, the Coming World Religion, by Arthur Findlay.
The Unfolding Universe, by Arthur Findlay.
The Way of Life, by Arthur Findlay.
The Psychic Stream: The Source or Growth of the Christian Faith, by Arthur Findlay.
The Torch of Knowledge, by Arthur Findlay.

Professor Archie Roy

Best of Both Worlds: A Tribute to a Great Medium (Albert Best), by Archie Roy.
Predictability, Stability, and Chaos in N-Body Dynamical Systems, by Archie E. Roy.
Long-Term Dynamical Behaviour of Natural and Artificial N-Body Systems, by Archie E. Roy.
From Newton to Chaos, by Archie E. Roy.
Archives of the Mind, by Archie E. Roy.
Things You Can Do When You're Dead, by Tricia J. Robertson.
More Things You Can Do When You're Dead, by Tricia J. Robertson.
It's Life and Death – but not as you know it, by Tricia J. Robertson.

Further Reading: The Pioneer Journal (Spiritualists' National Union)

All editions are free (online) and are compiled and researched by Paul J Gaunt, who is curator and librarian of the Britten Museum and Library at the Arthur Findlay College.

The journals will introduce you to even more pioneers of Spiritualism.

Website: www.pauljgaunt.com

Email: pioneer@snu.org.uk

Printed in Great Britain
by Amazon